HUNTING WITH THE MICROSCOPE

HUNTING WITH THE MICROSCOPE

Gaylord Johnson and Maurice Bleifield
revised by Joel Beller

ARCO PUBLISHING, INC.
NEW YORK

Third Edition, Third Printing, 1985

Published by Arco Publishing, Inc.
219 Park Avenue South, New York, N.Y. 10003

Library of Congress Cataloging in Publication Data

Johnson, Gaylord.
Hunting with the microscope.

SUMMARY: Discusses the selection of a microscope and describes procedures for using it to examine a wide variety of plant and animal specimens.
1. Microscope and microscopy—Juvenile literature. [1. Microscope and microscopy] I. Bleifeld, Maurice, joint author. II. Beller, Joe L. III. Title.

QH278.J63 1979 578 79-10291
ISBN 0-668-04973-1 (Library Edition)
ISBN 0-668-04783-6 (Paper Edition)

Printed in the United States of America

CONTENTS

HUNTING WITH THE MICROSCOPE

I

HOW TO USE THE "POCKET LENS"—SIMPLEST MICROSCOPE OF ALL

Right at the beginning I want to exercise the author's privilege of giving unasked advice.

It's a warning. Here it is:

If you think you "can't afford a microscope," don't start playing with a pocket lens!

Before you know it, you'll catch "microscopitis," and there is no cure, except the possession of a really good compound microscope.

If you are ready to take the risk, I'll proceed to show you a few of the fascinating ways in which you can use even the cheapest, most ordinary magnifying glass to hunt wonders in the sub-size world.

The enticing thing about microscope hunting is that its achievements are progressive—and so are its thrills. You can begin with a pocket "linen tester" lens, and have a whale of a good time with it until you can acquire, perhaps, a "fountain pen" pocket microscope, giving you an enlargement of 30 or 40 times. Your next jump after that will be to an instrument magnifying 100 to 200 diameters.

TYPES OF LENSES FOR VARIED USES

The ideal magnifier can't be bought because it is impossible to make. The perfect magnifier would be light in weight, yet sturdy. It would provide a wide field of view and magnify greatly. You can buy a magnifier with a large diameter lens that will give a large viewing area, but it has low magnifying power. A magnifier with a small diameter lens will have a higher magnification but will offer a smaller field of view. The field of view for a 5-power lens is about 40 mm. The field seen through a 10-power lens will be about 13 mm. In order to provide more viewing area and

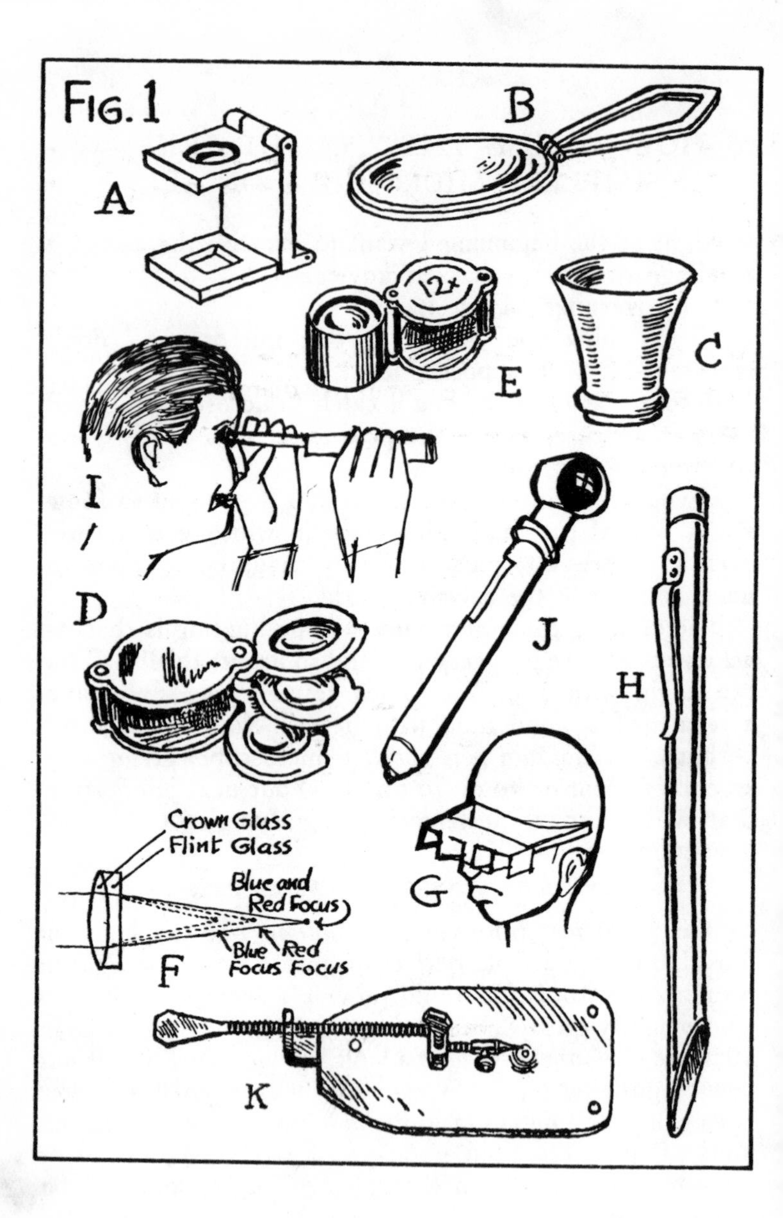
FIG. 1
A
B
12x
C
E
I
J
H
D
Crown Glass
Flint Glass
Blue and
Red Focus
Blue
Focus
Red
Focus
G
F
K

high magnification, a complex, heavy, high-cost lens system is needed. That is what the microscope is all about.

The facing page of sketches shows a few ot the forms the simple microscope or pocket magnifier may take. The following paragraphs will help you select the tool most suitable for you to start enjoying the pleasures of exploring the universe of the tiny.

A. *The Linen Tester.* As its name indicates, this is intended to count the number of threads per centimeter in linen or other fabrics. It magnifies about five diameters, and its base has engraved lines for easy counting of the number of threads.

We have mentioned the word *diameters,* so it would be a good idea to stop right here and make its meaning clear. If you look at the 1 mm. divisions on a ruler with a lens that magnifies four diameters, the width of one line seen through the lens would appear to be equal to the width of four lines side by side as seen with the unaided eye. *Four diameters magnification* or simply *4X* means that the object seen through the magnifier is four times as wide and four times as long as it appears without the magnifying glass.

In the advertising of cheap microscopes, you sometimes read that an instrument "magnifies over 1,000 times," or something equally amazing. The figure refers of course to the "surface area" of the magnified object, obtained by multiplying the width-enlargement by the length-enlargement. The actual magnification in diameters is therefore in this case only about 32.

B. *Folding Pocket Lens.* A convenient type to carry constantly in your pocket to inspect small objects in a general way. These folding lenses vary in power from 3 to 5 diameters. Their main advantage is the large field. They are really only reading glasses in miniature. A case is provided so that the lens will not become scratched.

C. *Watchmakers' "Loupe" or Eye-glass.* This is simply a three- or four-power lens of short focus, mounted into a plastic tube for holding in the eye, like a monocle, in order to leave both hands free for watch-repair work. This lens is sometimes a convenience when examining flowers or insects. The object can be held in one hand and manipulated with the other while the eyesocket holds the magnifier.

D. *Multiple Folding Pocket Magnifier.* This type consists of two or three lenses that are meant to be used singly or in combination. When not in use, they fold into the handle. This looks, at first sight, like a convenient arrangement, but will be found to be clumsy and irritating in use. It is much better to carry a wide-field, lower-power lens of three or four diameters for getting a general look and another smaller, high-power lens of ten or twelve diameters for detail work.

E. *Folding High Power Lens.* Most of the fine opticians put out their higher power magnifiers in some form similar to this. This type of magnifier varies from 5X to 20X, and sometimes even 30X. Lenses of these powers must, of course, be corrected for color. They must be *achromatic*, literally without color.

Let's take a short detour and see what *achromatism* means to our seeing ability. If you take a single lens (one made from a single piece of glass), say a reading glass, and strain it to the limit of its magnifying power, you'll see a fringe of orange and blue around the object at which you are looking. This indicates that the spectrum-colored rays making up the light are bent unequally by the passage through the lens, just as they are through a prism. This effect is not seriously detrimental to the efficiency of a three- or four-diameter magnifier, but in a ten- or twelve-power lens the rays are bent in so much more in the higher magnification that the color fringes become a real problem. Accordingly, all higher power magnifiers are *achromatic* or have *double* lenses. The diagram at F in *Figure 1* shows how the bending of the colored rays caused by a lens of one kind of glass is corrected by a lens made from another kind of glass (one with different light-bending power).

G. *Flip-up Binocular Magnifier.* Although these magnify only 2.5 diameters or so, the binocular magnifier is comfortable and easy to use. Squinting is unnecessary. Their main advantage is having both eyes magnified, thus seeing in three dimensions; that is, depth as well as length and width. The lenses can be flipped for normal vision. Delicate and precision work can be carried on since both hands are free.

H. *Fountain Pen Type Magnifier.* This type of hand lens really falls into the class of the compound microscope, for it is not one lens but two. The lens nearer your eye magnifies the image formed by the lens nearer the object. However, this magnifier is included here because it is carried and used as a pocket lens, being only about 25X to 50X in power. This type of instrument is excellent because it does not require the object to be held as close to the eye as a folding lens of corresponding magnification.

I. *Combined Telescope and Magnifier.* Here is an ingenious device which can be used either as a telescope or a microscope. When used as a microscope, it can magnify more than 50 diameters. The eyepiece must be drawn out when it is used as a telescope and the object will appear to be approximately ten times closer. This optical instrument is about 12 cm. in length and has a clip on it so it can be conveniently carried in your pocket. It is good both for examining small objects and for looking at a distant view. This type cannot, however, take the place of a good high-power pocket magnifier of the type shown at E in *Figure 1*.

J. *Illuminated Magnifier.* This optical instrument differs from all the other magnifiers we have discussed in that it has its own light source built into the handle. A small penlight battery supplies the power. The lens magnifies ten diameters. Its chief advantage is that the lens can be used when the lighting conditions are poor. Many types of illuminated magnifiers are manufactured for a variety of purposes. You can purchase a large field illuminated magnifier powered by two batteries or an illuminated magnifier with a fine focus adjustment that can magnify 30 diameters.

K. *The First Microscope.* This type of magnifier is illustrated here merely to show that one of the earliest microscopes perfected by Leeuwenhoek of Holland in the late 17th century was really nothing more than a single pocket lens. Focusing was done with a screw that regulated the distance between the lens and the object. This tiny lens was mounted between two thin plates. The object, placed on the point of a needle, was viewed through an opening scarcely larger than a pinhole. By thus restricting the opening of the lens, Leeuwenhoek was able to do away with the color fringes to a great extent. He constructed this type of microscope with lenses varying in power from 50 to 150 diameters, and with them made many of the pioneer discoveries in the microscopic science. Needless to say, he ground all his own lenses.

WHAT YOU CAN SEE WITH A POCKET LENS

I might fill this part of the chapter entirely with the names and descriptions of objects in which your pocket lens will reveal new and unsuspected interests and beauties. There is really no end to the fascinating revelations you can enjoy with only a modest-powered glass of 10 or 12 diameters.

The stinging hairs on a nettle leaf—the mould on damp bread—the spiral drinking proboscis of a moth or butterfly—the leg of a bee, with its wonderful "baskets" for carrying pollen—the tongue of a bee—the wings of insects—the noise apparatus of a house-cricket—the eggs of many different sorts of insects—the stamens

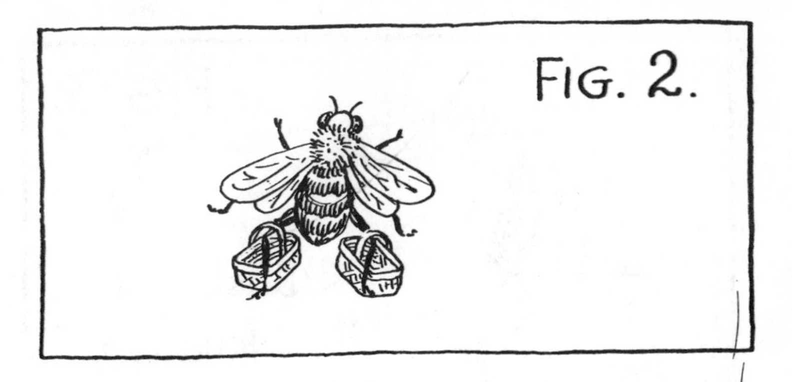

and pistils of flowers—these are only a few of the thousands of objects in which the owner of a good pocket lens can discern marvelous structures and mechanisms.

I might, as I say, describe some of them—but it would make dull reading—and I shall not do it. Instead, I am giving you as many simple sketches as I can of some of these objects which invite your scrutiny through the pocket lens—your "sharper eye." It will be much more fun for you than reading what they look like—and, still better, you'll know what you're looking for.

Here's an instance of what I mean: If I tell you that the honey bee has a "market basket" upon each of her hind legs, you will probably think of a picture something like *Figure 2*. That is absurd of course. But if I draw you a fairly *true* picture of the way the bee's "basket" really looks, as in *Figure 3*, you will look at the next bee you see upon a flower with a thrill of real expectancy. You will then know what to look for; you will be curious to see the basket for yourself, and eager to point it out to others.

There is the "basket," stuffed full of the yellow pollen dust. How firmly the curving, springy hairs hold in the little yellow mass of sticky golden "flour" that is

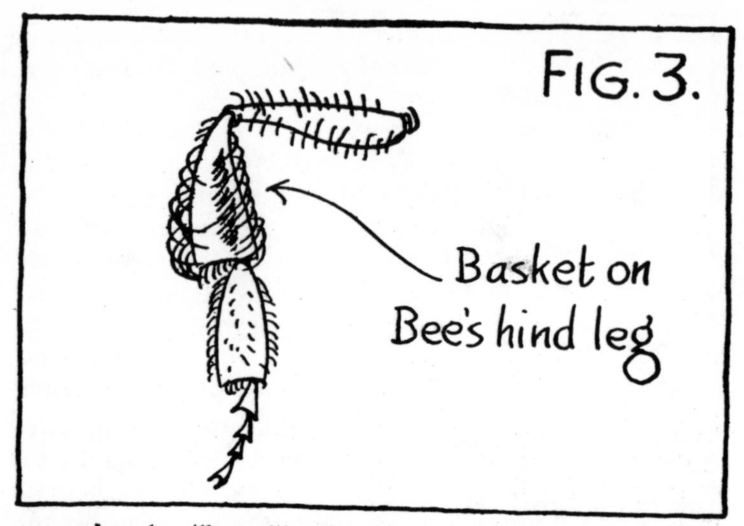

to make the "bread" of baby bees in the home hive! Even while you watch through a reading glass lens, the bee (oblivious of your scrutiny) is using her fore-legs to pack still more into the tiny receptacle. Do you wonder that this wonderful device is called a "basket?"

Scores of visual adventures like this await you and your two lenses—the wide-field one for examining scenes "in action," and the shorter-focused, more powerful one for examining the structures of the insect you have caught and killed. You can do this easily in a wide-mouthed bottle with a little household ammonia absorbed into a circle of blotting paper on the bottom. In a few minutes the insect is dead, and ready for detailed examination.

With your pocket lenses to aid your own sight, you can at once start out upon a journey into a country that is strange and new, but not far away. Step into the nearest garden, field or city park, and you are at once in the center of this unexplored territory—this land of little things. But nature finishes the tiniest insect with most exquisite care. In the jaws, legs and eyes of the first grasshopper or dragon fly you catch, your lens will reveal a beauty and ingenuity which will fascinate you with their wonder.

The best service I can do you now is to provide some pictures which indicate the features you should look for in the structures of insects—for these offer one of the most interesting of all fields for the pocket lens, just as the minute life of a pond offers the best objects for the compound microscope. We will investigate this later.

For the sake of the remarkable contrasts to be noted, we shall look at the same structure or organ as found in several different insects. For example, the pictures in *Figure 4* show the interesting differences to be noted between the *eyes* of several different creatures. In the same way, *Figure 5* represents the varieties to be seen in *legs* and *Figures 6* and *7* show the styles in *mouths*.

The pictures are the important things, but I am going to make a few running comments on them as we go along.

A in Figure 4. One of the most wonderful pairs of eyes in the whole world belongs to the dragon fly, and he has also a most wonderful set of wings. (These two facts go together, as you will see.) The dragon fly is almost never still. He will not stay to be examined. He must be caught in an insect net, and popped into the ammonia bottle until he is dead and quiet. Then you can look at his wonderful eyes through your lens.

Can it be that those two great dark rounding masses that meet on top of the head and extend forward and down on each side of the mouth are really eyes? They cover nearly the entire head, or at least two-thirds of it!

When the dragon fly poises motionless for a second in the air, like a humming bird, his great search-lights of eyes look north, south, east and west, above and below—all ways at once. He can see his prey in any direction, and his powerful wings take him instantly in pursuit.

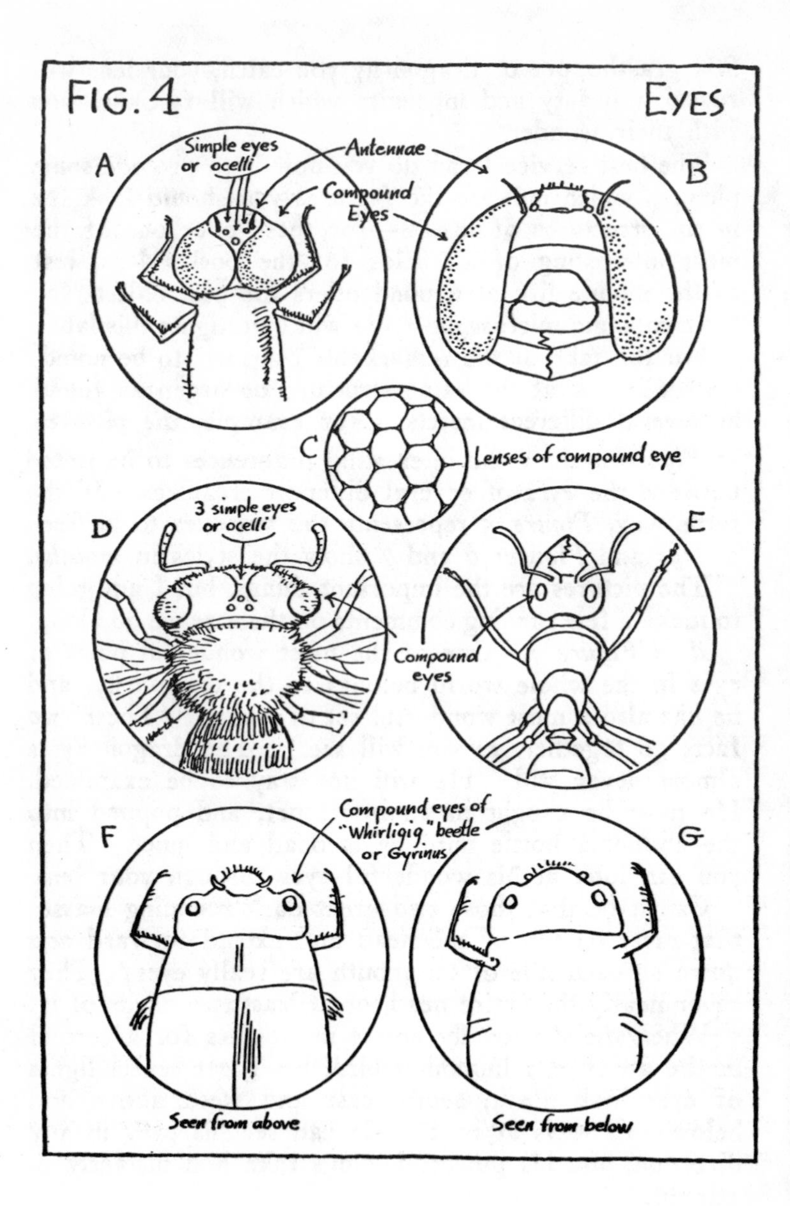
FIG. 4
EYES
A
Simple eyes
or ocelli
Antennae
Compound
Eyes
B
C
Lenses of compound eye
D
3 simple eyes
or ocelli
E
Compound
eyes
F
Compound eyes of
"Whirligig" beetle
or Gyrinus
G
Seen from above
Seen from below

Now look through your lens again at the top of the dragon fly's head. What do you see in that triangular space between the two great curving eyes? Two short, pointed horns or feelers—and three little round dots or knobs, close under the edge of the big eyes. The three little knobs are also eyes, but simple ones.

Now turn the creature so that his mouth faces you. *B in Figure 4.* Observe the surface of the great eyes closely. It is dull, not shiny black. With a pocket lens magnifying only 5 diameters, you cannot see that the whole area of both eyes is covered with a myriad of little six-sided dots. But with a lens magnifying 20 times or more, you could see them quite plainly. They look like the ends of the cells in a honey bee's comb. What are they? Eyes, every one! Each of the tiny hexagons, which look, under a microscope, something like *C in Figure 4,* has a lens and an optic nerve and makes a clear picture of what is directly in front of it. We know this because miniature photographs have been taken with these lenses.

D in Figure 4. After looking so carefully at the head of the dragon fly, you quickly recognize all the same parts in the bee's head. You see the large compound eyes, the three little black knobs, or simple eyes, and the feelers or antennae.

They are the same in a general way, but very different in detail. The eyes are not great half-globes covering nearly all the head, but more moderate in size, and placed wide apart. They are strangely hairy too. The little simple eyes are more prominent and the feelers much larger.

Here again nature has supplied the creature with exactly the kind of tools needed for its life, for the bee makes great use of her feelers, and does not really need such all-seeing eyes as the fierce, meat-hunting dragon fly does.

E in Figure 4. Now let us take one of the large black ants which are crossing our path. We will interrupt her business long enough to have a look at her head. If you pick her up carefully, you can hold her quiet in your fingers without killing her in the ammonia bottle.

What a strange looking head! What large feelers! What prominent jaws! And the eyes, how comparatively small they are, sitting on each side of the black head. The ant's eyes are large enough, of course, to be very useful, but, since it walks every where as a rule instead of flying, it has many more opportunities to use a good pair of feelers. So they grow very large. The ant not only feels with them, but probably also smells with them, and most certainly talks to other ants with them. With all these uses for her antennae, it is no wonder that nature makes them grow large, many-jointed and pliable.

F in Figure 4. A few steps down our road the surface of a pond is rippling in the breeze. What are those shiny little black things circling round each other so rapidly near shore? "Whirligig Beetles," and well named. The scientific name is *Gyrinus,* which is related to "gyrate." Catch one in your pond-net. It looks like a small black bean of some kind. Pick it up gently between your thumb and finger and have a look at its head through your lens. Look at it first from above.

The whirligig's large eyes are wide apart, but still some distance from the margin of its head. They do not curve down over the sides, as in the bee and dragon fly.

Now turn the little beetle over and look carefully at its underside, the side that is in contact with the water when it is rushing in rapid circles. Remarkably enough, the whirligig seems to have another pair of eyes upon the under-side of its head, a pair of "water telescopes," so that no matter how the breeze stirs the surface, or how many ripples it makes itself, it can always see its

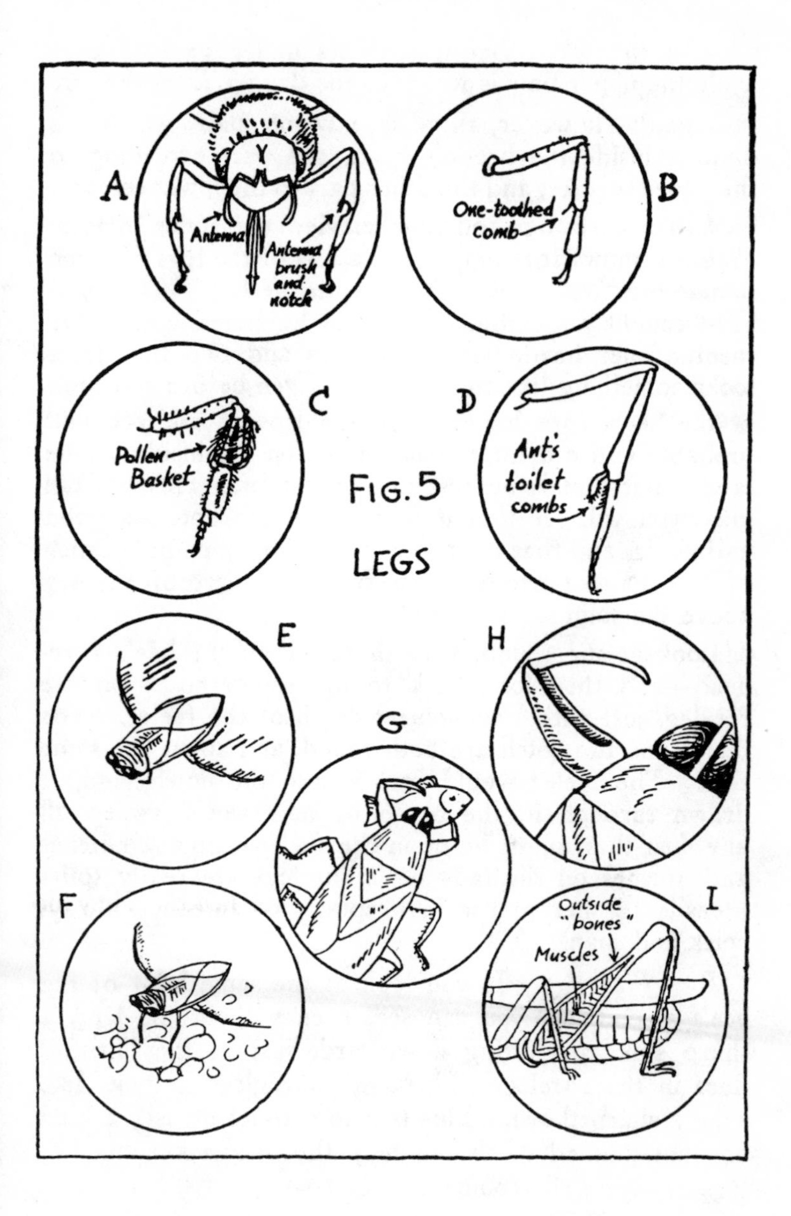
A
Antenna
Antenna brush and notch
B
One-toothed comb
C
Pollen Basket
D
Ant's toilet combs
FIG. 5
LEGS
E
H
G
F
I
Outside "bones"
Muscles

prey in the water below with its under pair of eyes while the upper pair is watching for danger from the air.

Actually, however, there is only *one* pair, which are divided inside the beetle's head, one part extending to the upper surface, and the other part to the lower surface.

A in Figure 5. And now to view the styles in legs. *Figure 5* shows for comparison a few of the legs of some common insects. Let us begin with the bee. After you have caught and killed one in an ammonia bottle, the front of her head, with its feelers and two fore legs, looks something like this picture. Even before you look at the bee's fore leg through the lens at all, you will probably notice a little round notch on the inside of the large joint that is nearest the bee's foot. Through the glass you will see that it is quite a deep notch, a good half-circle, and that over it a little spike or pointed brush of stiff hairs projects down from the part of the leg above the joint.

Look at the round, smooth feeler on the bee's forehead—and then look back to the round notch on the foreleg, just within convenient reach of the feeler. The feeler and the notch are both round, and about the same size. The feeler would just fit into the notch, and, if drawn through it, the brush of hair would sweep off any dust that might be upon the feeler. So the notches and brushes on the lady bee's forelegs are really toilet utensils for her to use in keeping her antennae always spick and span.

B in Figure 5. If you look at the same joint of the bee's second leg, you can see, even without the lens, a sharp spike projecting downward, just as the "brush" does in the foreleg. Through your glass it looks like a long sharp thorn. This is also a toilet utensil, a kind of "one-toothed comb" to help the bee in keeping her legs always well-groomed.

C in Figure 5. Looking at the hind leg. You see how the limb is made broad and flat in order to provide a wide bottom for the basket; and how the sides, formed of stiff, springy hairs, curve up over the wide groove in the middle section of the leg. Next time you see a bee on a sunflower (which furnishes her with an abundance of pollen) notice how full these baskets can be stuffed without spilling their loads.

Now we shall need to pay another visit to the pond where we caught our "whirligig" when we were comparing the eyes of insects. We will take our dip net, and an ordinary tumbler in which to observe the working of a very remarkable pair of legs.

But on the way to the pond let us once more pick up a large ant, hold her under the lens and see if she has any leg-devices as clever and useful as the bee's.

D in Figure 5. Ants are just as neat as bees! The pocket-lens shows that the ant also has an "antenna cleaner," in the same joint of the foreleg where the bee carries hers. But it is not a groove and brush this time, but two little combs. The ant draws her feelers through these two combs just as the bee pulls hers through the groove-and-brush cleaner. Set the ant down on the road again and let us see what strange kinds of legs await us in the pond.

E in Figure 5. Stoop down and look sharply into the shallows near shore. Perhaps you will see a creature that has a very remarkable pair of legs indeed. Ah, he is really there! Do you see that little seed-shaped thing, less than half-an-inch long, advancing through the water by jerks? Indeed he *is rowing*—just like a man in a boat! No wonder he is called the "water-boatman." Scoop him up with the net and put him into the tumbler full of water with a few little pebbles in the bottom.

Then perhaps you can see those wonderful little "oars" with one of your lenses.

Do you see those fringes of hair along the edges of his "oars?" As the oar comes forward, toward the head, the hairs are drawn forward limply, without making any resistance. But when the "water boatman" makes his "stroke," the hairs spread out, thrusting backward powerfully, and the boat leaps ahead.

F in Figure 5. Now the insect has come to rest for a moment. His long middle pair of legs are grasping one of the little pebbles in the bottom of the tumbler. The front pair are tucked up under the head. The "oars" are spread out on either side. This is how the water boatman looks when at rest.

Probably he was originally equipped with six legs, but, when his ancestors took to the water, two of them became adapted for swimming, the others being used for walking and standing.

Another pond insect has learned the same lesson of economy. This is the Giant Water Bug, called "Belostoma" by scientific men.

Sweep your net around over the pond bottom under those weeds near shore, and see whether you have luck. If you do, you won't be in doubt, for Belostoma deserves his name—he is sometimes over three inches long!

Up with the net—and there, in the midst of the dead leaves and trash, is a fair-sized Belostoma—and he is eating a baby sun-fish only an inch long!

G in Figure 5. You do not need a magnifying glass to see how he does it. He has seized the baby fish with his strong, tong-like claws. With them he is holding the prey close under his head, while he sucks the fish's blood through the sharp, strong beak that is plunged deep into its flesh. In handling the giant water bug you must have a care, for he can inflict a painful sting in your finger with that same beak.

I said a moment ago that Nature had made Belostoma learn the same lesson of economy that the water boatman had learned. You see at once that the giant bug has only four legs to walk with. The pair of tongs holding the baby fish is the other pair of legs—useless now for walking, but very useful to Belostoma for seizing his dinner as it swims past!

H in Figure 5. If you look through the lens at one of the tongs, you will see that the thick, heavy part has a groove, in the side next the head. Into this groove the smaller, sharp-pointed part of the tong folds. It fits into the thick part as the blade of your pocket knife closes into its handle.

I in Figure 5. There goes a locust, wrongly called a "grasshopper" by some people. Watch where he lands, and sweep the insect net down over the spot. You have him. Take him out and look at his wonderful leaping legs with your pocket lens.

How thick and muscular the part nearest his body is! The pretty pattern on the side of the limb shows where the big leaping muscles are. Those little diamond-shaped spaces are their ends. Along the sides of this patterned surface run two strong, curved bands. They form a sort of oval picture-frame around the muscles; then they join together and make the joint for the straight, stiff part of the leg.

In *your* leg the muscles are attached to bones which run *inside,* through the center. They are deep out of sight. But in the locust's leg, the "bones" are *outside.* It is the same with the bee, the ant and other insects. They have no backbone, no inside skeleton. The supporting frame-work of an insect is always outside, in plain sight.

Are the different kind of mouths that insects eat with

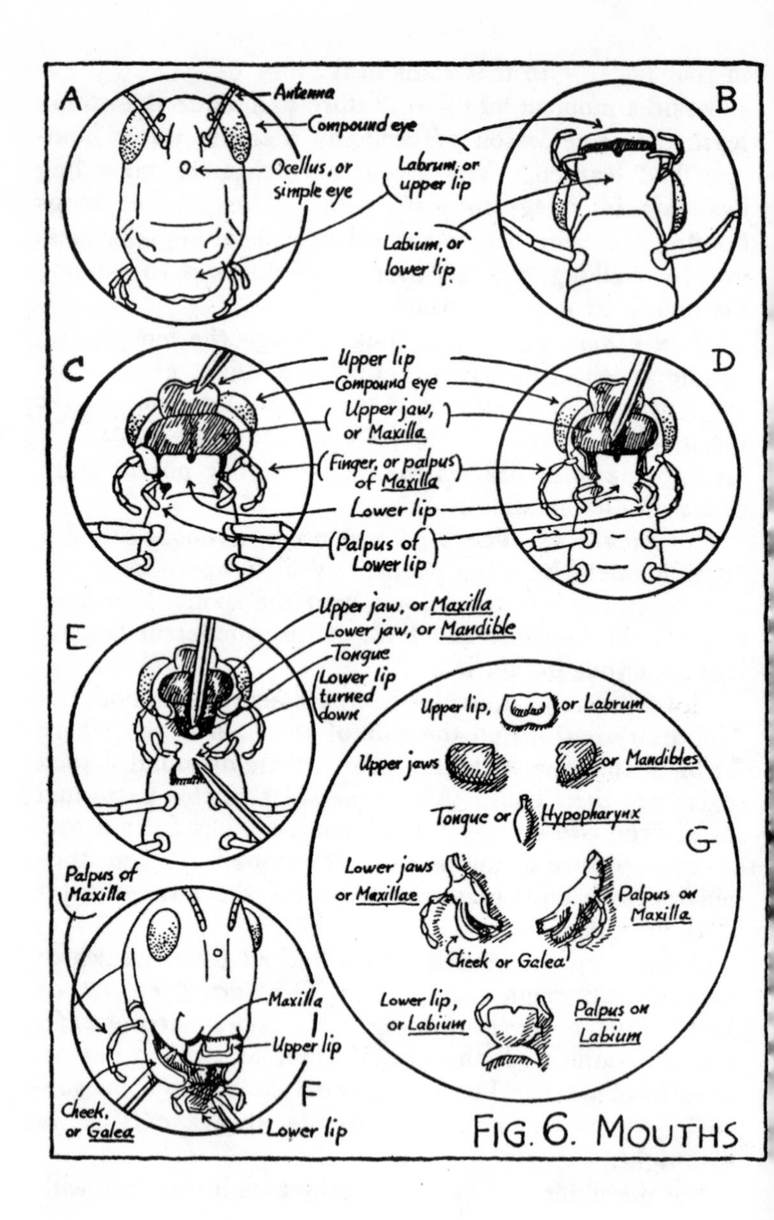
A
B
C
D
E
F
G
Antenna
Compound eye
Ocellus, or simple eye
Labrum, or upper lip
Labium, or lower lip
Upper lip
Compound eye
Upper jaw, or Maxilla
Finger, or palpus of Maxilla
Lower lip
Palpus of Lower lip
Upper jaw, or Maxilla
Lower jaw, or Mandible
Tongue
Lower lip turned down
Upper lip, or Labrum
Upper jaws or Mandibles
Tongue or Hypopharynx
Lower jaws or Maxillae
Palpus on Maxilla
Cheek or Galea
Lower lip, or Labium
Palpus on Labium
Palpus of Maxilla
Maxilla
Upper lip
Cheek, or Galea
Lower lip

FIG. 6. MOUTHS

as interesting and wonderful as the varieties of eyes and legs? Yes, and you will be able to investigate them yourself—with your pocket lens. The pages of pictures in *Figures 6 and 7* will serve as your guide and show you what to look for with your lens.

Figure 6 will show how you can use a common locust or "grasshopper" to learn the principal parts of a typical insect's mouth. Then *Figure 7* will give you an exercise in identifying these various parts under a number of strange and remarkable "disguises."

Just a few running comments on these two pages of pictures, and then we must get into the next chapter and consider the "compound" microscope, which you may already be impatient to investigate.

A in Figure 6. The locust has the best mouth to start with. What a strange face! A little like the head of a "bock beer" goat. You notice at once the large compound eyes, the ocelli, and the antennae. Where are the mouth parts we are going to examine carefully with our pocket lens?

There, at the lower end of the locust's face, is something that looks like an upper lip. Insert the point of a pin under it and see if it moves. It is not of flexible, soft flesh, like your lips. Rather it is quite stiff and horny, but it can be moved up and down upon the hinge that joints it to the face.

B in Figure 6. Now let us find the other parts of the mouth. What about the locust's jaws? How are they different from ours? Let us see. Take the pin again. Lift up the upper lip and hold it. What is that shiny, dark brown mass that is revealed?

It must be the locust's upper jaw. See if you can find the teeth. They are not where you would expect to find them, are they? But the jagged line running across the brown mass from upper to lower lip looks like two rows of saw-teeth meeting. Try to insert the point of the pin into this line, and see what happens.

D in Figure 6. The pin makes the hard, dark mass divide; the two halves move apart sideways! It is plain that the locust's jaws are not like ours, opening and closing up and down. Instead, they open out to right and left. The teeth, too, you notice, are not set into the jaw, like those of animals, but are merely sharp points of the jaw itself.

E in Figure 6. Now, while you hold the jaws apart with your pin, watch through the lens while I take another pin and turn down the flap-like lower lip. This reveals another pair of jaws—the lower pair, called the "mandibles." These are smaller, with fewer teeth on their edges. When you have pushed your pin a little farther down, this lower pair will also open up sidewise. Instead of two jaws, like ours, the locust has four—an upper pair, called the "maxillae," and this lower pair, the mandibles.

Just below and between the lower jaws, you will see the locust's tongue, called the "hypo-pharynx," projecting from the cavity of the mouth. Now we have found all the parts of the mouth—two lips, four jaws and a tongue, except one, the cheeks.

F in Figure 6. Turn the locust so that we can look at his head a little from one side. Then lift up, with a pin point, that little flexible flap that covers the side of the lower jaw.

That is the locust's "cheek," or "galea." It is really attached to the lower jaw.

Now that we have seen all the different parts of the locust's mouth, we are ready to try to recognize the same mouth parts in some other insects. It will not be easy, for we shall find them masquerading under many disguises.

G in Figure 6. Perhaps, however, it will be a good

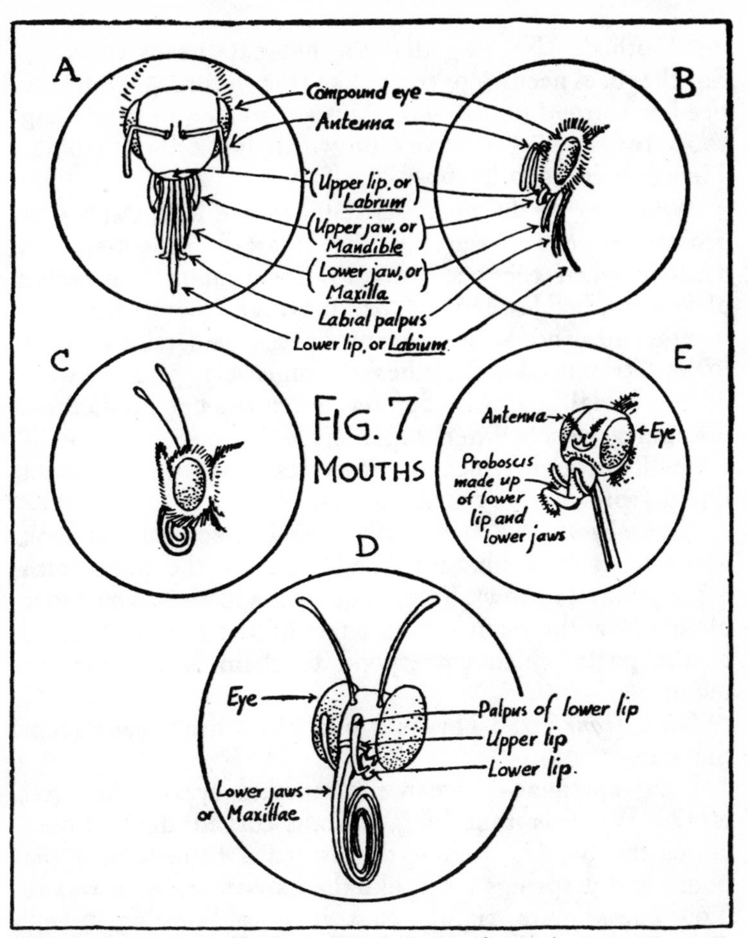

plan to remove all the parts of the locust's mouth and glue them firmly to a little card. Then we can see at a glance how the parts of the bee's or butterfly's mouth differ from the locust's. These variations to meet special needs are shown in *Figure 7*.

A in Figure 7. Here is a full-front view of the honey bee's face, as seen through your pocket lens. Notice that the edges of the mandibles, or upper jaws, are not toothed. Nothing that the bee eats needs chewing. So the bee needs no teeth like the locust's. But the bee has learned to use these jaws as molding or modelling tools for shaping the wax of which her cells are built. Hence their smooth, spoon-like form.

What can be the purpose of those five long parts that project down between the upper jaws? Scientists tell us that when the bee took to living upon the nectar of flowers, her lower jaws, or "maxillae," became greatly lengthened, and hollowed out on the undersides. The lower lip was also lengthened immensely, and so were its two labial "palpi." So now, when the bee holds these five parts closely fitted together, a long strong tube is formed, through which the insect can suck up the sweet liquid from the hearts of flowers.

B in Figure 7. If you turn the bee so you can look at its head from the side, and separate the parts with a pin point, as shown here, your lens will show you more plainly how the eight mouth parts of the bee are related to the parts which correspond to them in the locust's mouth.

C in Figure 7. This is a butterfly's head, seen from the side.

Long antennae—immense compound eyes—and what else? What is that long, spirally-curved dark thread under the head? Pull it downward a little with a pin point, and it springs back, like the hair-spring of a watch. You guess quite rightly that it is a "sucking tube," something like the proboscis of the bee, but you would never guess what mouth-parts have been changed and modified to form it.

Take the pin again and unroll the little spring to its ful length. See how long it is? It enables the butterfly to suck the nectar from deep, narrow flowers. Evidently the insect depends entirely upon its flexible soda-straw when it wants to eat.

D in Figure 7. It will be useless to guess at the identity of the parts that form it until we remove the coating

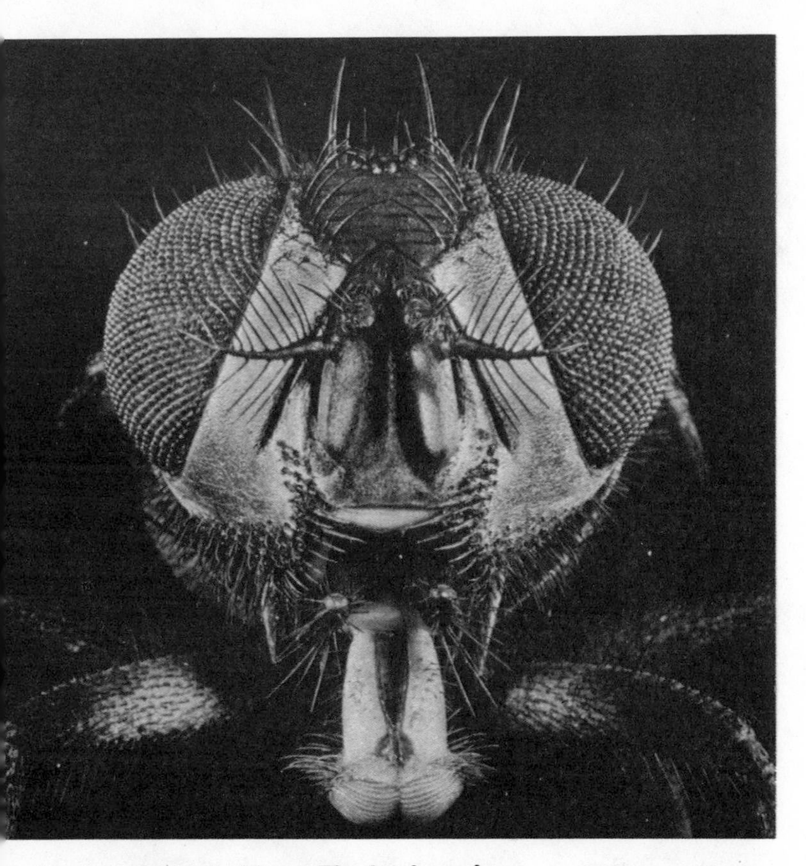

Fig. 8. Domestic House Fly, head-on view.
Courtesy of American Museum of Natural History

of fuzzy hairs which cover the whole head and face. By scraping carefully with the point of a sharp pen knife, and then using a very small, dry water-color brush, the hairs rub off easily. When the whole head and face are thoroughly cleaned, it will look like this through your pocket lens.

Now we see that the sucking-tube is made from the maxillae, the two lower jaws. They have been enormously lengthened, grooved on the inner sides, and fitted together to make a "soda straw" for the butterfly.

E in Figure 7. The common house fly is another insect which gets its food entirely by sucking up liquids. As a result of having no food that needs chewing, both its upper and lower jaws have practically disappeared. Take a look at its face through the lens, while you hold the proboscis, or sucking organ, extended downward with a pin. Notice that this kind of a sucking organ is devised to take liquids from flat, open surfaces, upon which the fly stands, while the butterfly's slender "hose-reel" is contrived so that it can reach down into the deepest, narrowest places in the blossoms of flowers, which flies never visit for food.

II

HOW MICROSCOPES MAKE TINY OBJECTS VISIBLE

To understand what the lens system in a compound microscope does, let's start with a familiar object, like a leaf from a household plant. Remove a leaf from a Coleus or Geranium and hold it at arm's length. Look at the underside. Notice the veins and other structures. Slowly bring the leaf toward your eye. As it gets closer, it gets bigger and you can see more detail. For most people, detail will be lost when the leaf is brought closer than 15 cm. The leaf will continue to be magnified but it will blur. Microscopes, on the other hand, preserve the detail while magnifying much more than the eye. This is shown in *Figure 9*.

If you are thinking of buying your own microscope, a cheap one that may magnify 700 diameters or more but fails to reveal detail is worthless. *Resolving Power* or the ability to reveal detail is just as important as magnifying power. Resolving power is the measure of the smallest distance between two closely spaced objects that shows them to be separate rather than being a single blurry object. The smaller the distance, the higher the resolving power. A good light microscope will reveal structures separated by as little as 0.2 μ (mu) apart. μ is the symbol for a *micron*, which is 1/1000 of a millimeter. The working limit for a compound microscope is 900X: Over 1000X, the image will appear dim and poorly defined. The limit on magnification is due to the wavelength of light. The rule is that the smaller the wavelength, the greater the magnification at which two adjacent dots can be seen as distinct and separate. For light, the maximum magnifying power is about 1500 diameters and this requires oil-immersion objectives and special techniques. For our purposes, a microscope that magnifies 400 diameters is sufficient.

Objects smaller than 0.2 microns cannot be resolved by

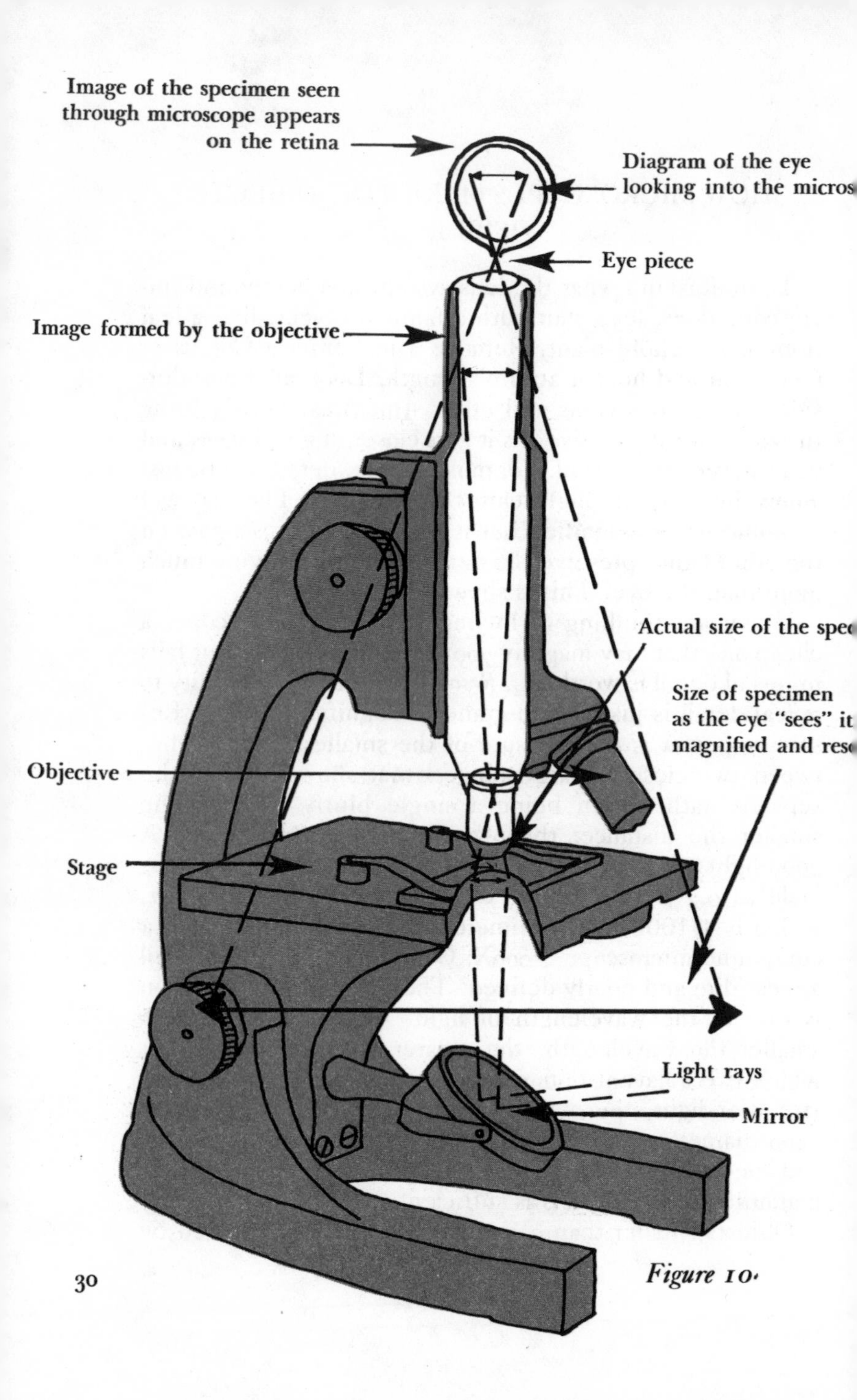
Image of the specimen seen
through microscope appears
on the retina
Diagram of the eye
looking into the micros
Eye piece
Image formed by the objective
Actual size of the spe
Size of specimen
as the eye "sees" it
magnified and res
Objective
Stage
Light rays
Mirror

Figure 10

the light microscope but they can be resolved by an *electron microscope.* This type of microscope uses a beam of electrons rather than light. Since the wavelength of electrons is so much smaller than the wavelength of light, details of structures 0.0002 microns apart can be seen when magnified up to 300,000X. There are two kinds of electron microscopes: the *transmission electron microscope* and the *scanning electron microscope.*

In both types of electron microscopes, the lenses are made of electromagnets instead of glass. A heated filament at one end produces the electrons which then move at high speed through a vacuum. They are gathered and focused by the electromagnetic lenses. The image appears in black and white, as seen in *Figure 10*. If there were molecules of air present instead of a vacuum, the electrons would be scattered upon striking the molecules and no meaningful image would be produced.

The specimen in the transmission electron microscope must be very thin, no more than 0.1 micron thick, in order to record an image on a fluorescent screen or photographic plate. The electrons will pass through some molecules of the specimen, striking the screen or photographic plate to yield the black part of the image. The white area is produced by the electrons that were scattered by the specimen and never reached the photographic plate or fluorescent screen.

In the scanning electron microscope, the image is produced by gathering the electrons that have bounced off the surface of the specimen. This means that the specimen can be very thick. A housefly could be placed in the specimen chamber and its surface structure viewed with the scanning electron microscope. Some scattered electrons bounce into the detector and produce a signal. That signal is then translated into a black and white picture of the surface of the specimen on the TV screen.

Both electron microscopes are compared to the light

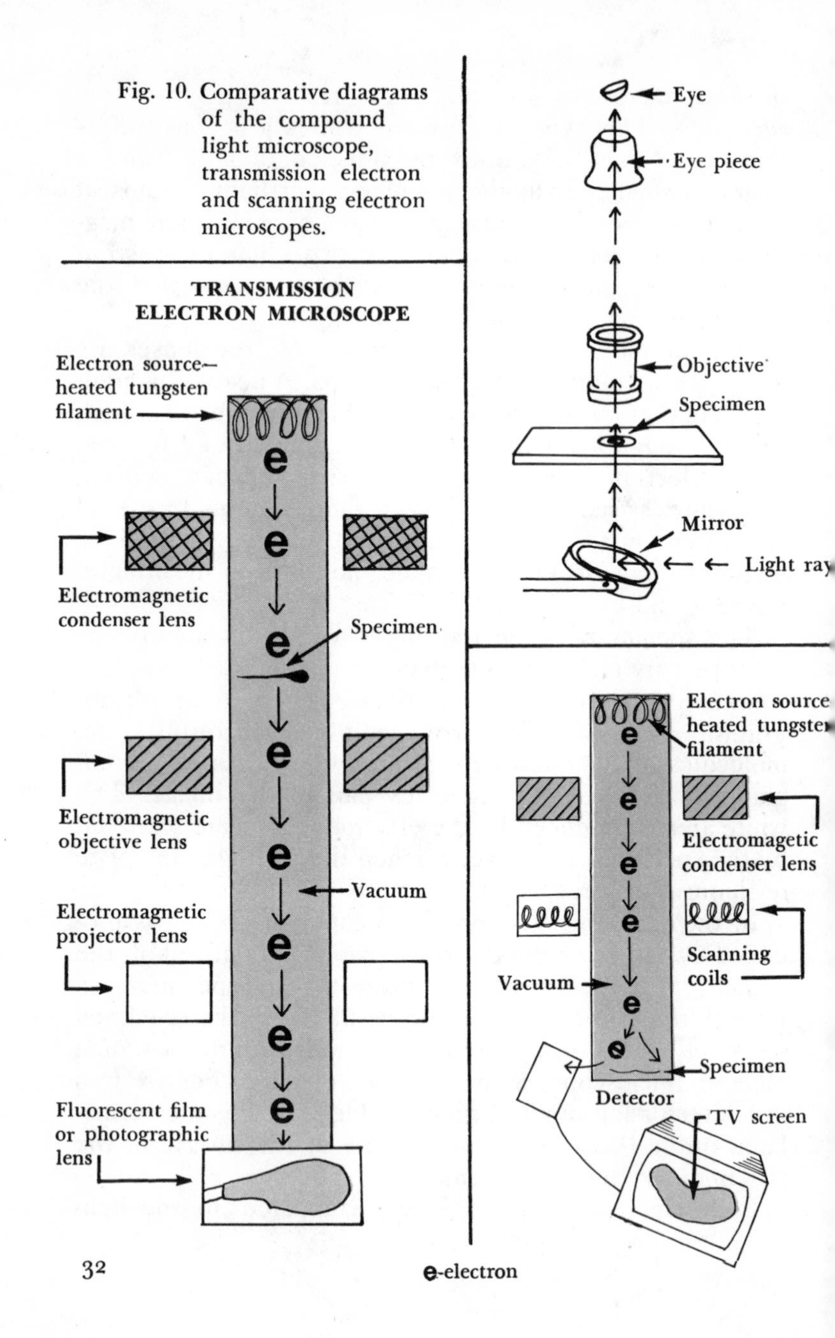

Fig. 10. Comparative diagrams of the compound light microscope, transmission electron and scanning electron microscopes.

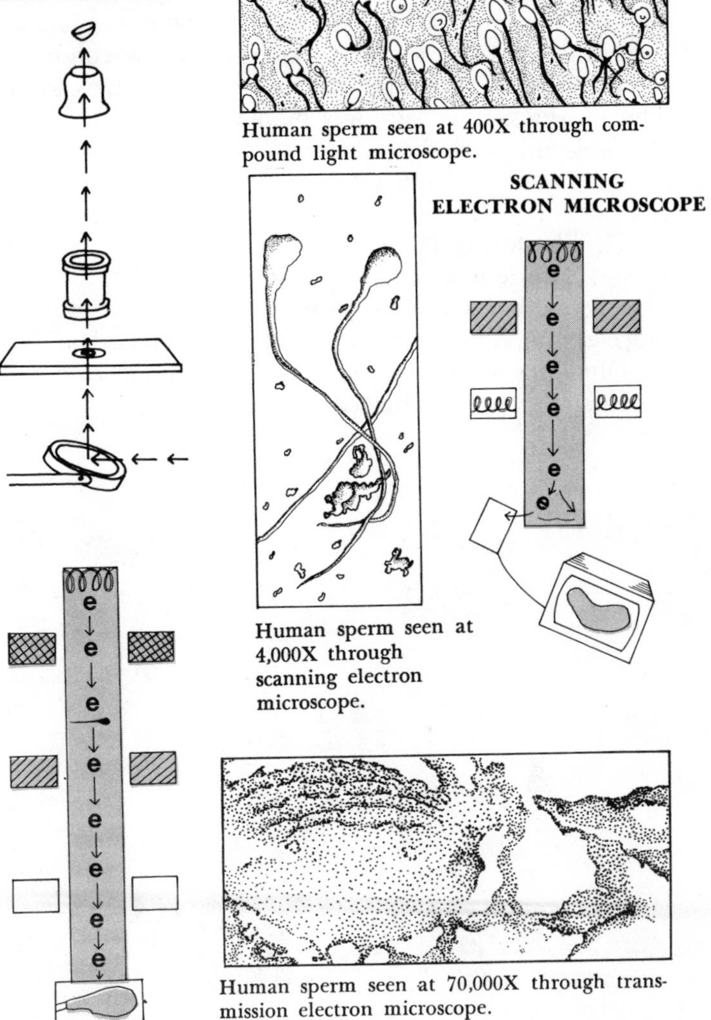

Human sperm seen at 400X through compound light microscope.

Human sperm seen at 4,000X through scanning electron microscope.

Human sperm seen at 70,000X through transmission electron microscope.

Fig. 11. Comparison of magnifications possible with compound and electron microscopes.

microscope in *Figure 10* and on the back cover. In this figure you can see that the electron microscopes are larger and more complicated than the compound microscope. This is because the electron microscopes are composed of three major systems: power, vacuum, and lens systems. The power system supplies high voltage to produce the electrons and work the vacuum pumps, lenses and controls. Several vacuum pumps work together and can produce very low vacuums in the column through which the electrons travel. The fewer molecules in the vacuum, the better the image. The lenses consist of magnetic fields produced by passing electric currents through wire coils surrounding a piece of iron. The electrons travel in a spiral path and not in straight lines as light does; however they are carefully focused and controlled by the lenses.

III

HOW TO CHOOSE AND HANDLE YOUR WEAPONS FOR HUNTING IN THE MICRO-JUNGLE

No experienced hunter would place a loaded shotgun in the hands of a person who had never fired one, and turn him loose in the woods. Accordingly, the first step in guiding you into the really thrilling pastime sport of hunting with the compound microscope will be a few words about the cautions to exercise in selecting and using one. You are already familiar with the use of the "hand" or "pocket" lens and its possibilities.

The great popularity of the microscope as a hobby has brought a great many instruments of all prices upon the market These are sold both singly and in the form of sets—including a microscope and various accessories in the form of a boxed outfit.

Some of these microscopes have merit, and others are mere toys—utterly useless. The lenses of the latter are so poorly ground that they will not give you a clear image at any magnification. To make them was a waste of time and material, and to give them to a boy or girl as an introduction to the pleasures of microscope-hunting is a crime.

Most of these toy instruments are so bad optically that their use is very hard on the eyes. But this is not their worst feature, for a boy or girl will quickly give up using such a poor instrument, thus removing this danger. The real offense in marketing such an "imitation" of a microscope is that the person who uses it in the freshness of his first enthusiasm is deeply disappointed, and naturally feels that the pleasures of microscope hunting have been much exaggerated. A worthless instrument thus frequently blocks the first eager steps in the path to a hobby which, with even a fairly good microscope might give both fun and instruction in increasing measure.

Like everything else you can't buy a good microscope for a little money. If you want to be reasonably sure of getting a good instrument, you're going to have to spend some money. The ideal microscope for the amateur who expects to take this hobby seriously is a student's microscope with a low and a high power objective. 10X is fine for the low power objective and around 40X for the high power. Using an eyepiece that magnifies 10 diameters, you will achieve a magnification of 100 diameters with the low power and 400 diameters with the high power. The reason for the increase is that the image you see is an image of an image!

The image formed by the objective is re-magnified by the eyepiece (see *Figure 9*). The magnifying power of any microscope is the result of multiplying the magnifying power of the objective by the magnifying power of the eyepiece.

The objectives of your microscope should be *parfocal*. This means that when you change from one objective to the other, the image will remain in almost perfect focus, needing only a little turning of the fine adjustment knob.

A diaphragm under the stage is an essential part of your first microscope. It regulates the amount of light entering the microscope.

For more money you can purchase a student microscope with a built-in light source and a condenser under the stage, in addition to the diaphragm. When using the high power objective the condenser is extremely helpful because it converges the parallel rays of light that enter the microscope to provide enough light to see the specimen clearly.

If you have even more money to spend, you can purchase a microscope with a zoom optical system that provides continuous varying magnification that is always in focus. Similar optical systems are used on the sporting events you see on TV. The TV camera is able to zoom in for a close-up

BRISTOL COMPOUND MICROSCOPE

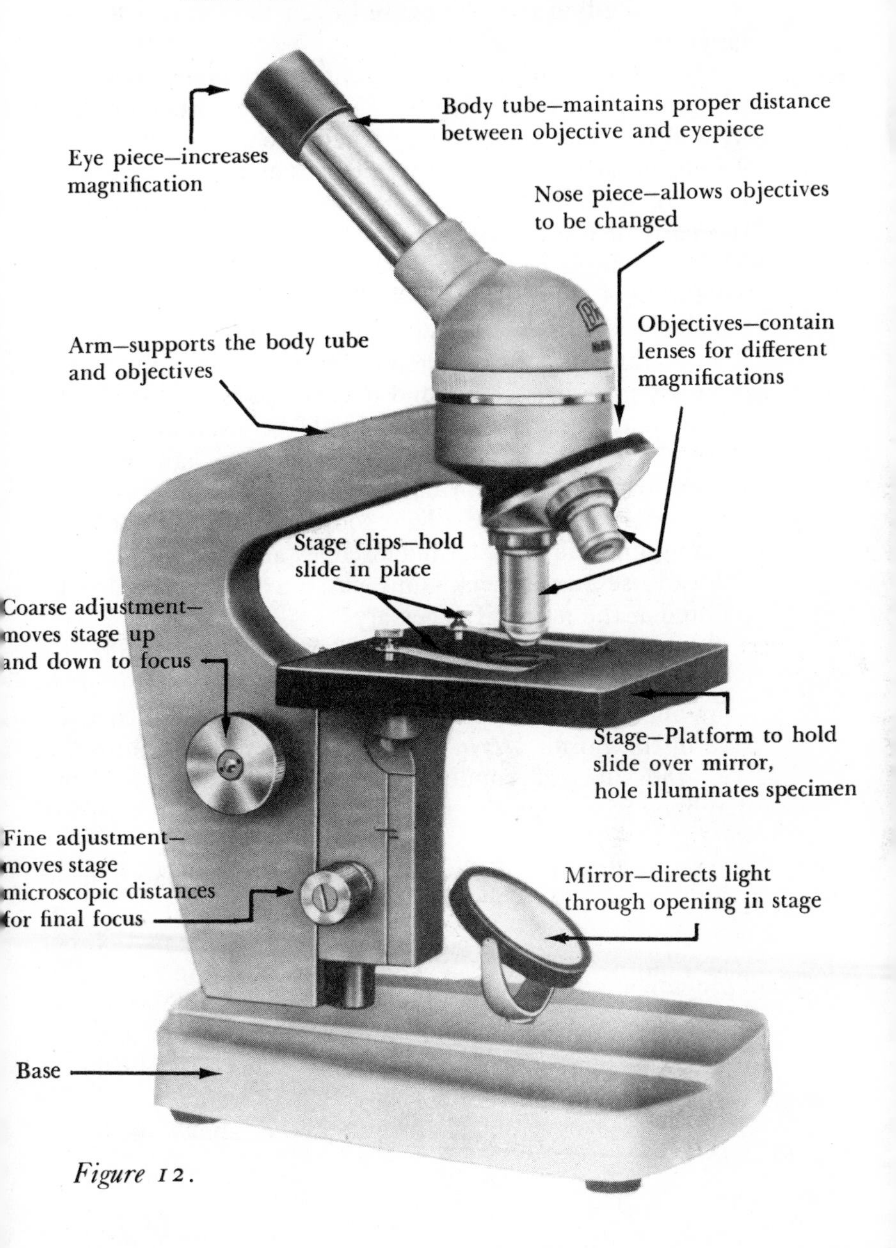

Figure 12.

without needing to be refocused even though it is located far away.

Second-hand microscopes are cheaper than new ones and will work just as well, provided the adjustments move easily and the lenses are not scratched. Look carefully at the visible surfaces of the objective lenses and the eyepiece. If they are scratched, *don't buy it!* If you are unfamiliar with the parts of the microscope, they are shown in *Figure 12*. Most beginners have trouble with two procedures: adjusting the light and focusing.

Let's first discuss lighting. The importance of proper illumination cannot be overemphasized, for without proper light even the best compound microscope is useless. Artificial light rather than daylight should be used at all times since the amount and intensity of artificial light will not change with the time of day or the weather. This is why many microscopes have a light source built into their base. Although illuminators for microscopes are relatively cheap, you can use a gooseneck lamp with a 25-watt frosted bulb pointed at the mirror if necessary.

Note that the mirror is flat (plane) on one side while the center appears to be pushed in (concave) on the other. If your microscope has no condenser, then use the concave side of the mirror. *Always* use the plane side of the mirror with the substage condenser. By varying the size of the diaphragm opening, you can get the correct amount of light.

Always clean the lenses and mirror with lens paper made especially for this purpose. Even though they are soft, tissues should not be used because they leave tiny particles of paper on the glass that show up as part of the image.

Focusing the microscope is a simple process, but must be done carefully. Begin by centering the slide over the opening in the stage. The stage opening must be well illuminated by your light source. Now, lower the low power objective until it is about six millimeters above the slide.

Look through the eyepiece and slowly turn the coarse adjustment knob *toward* you. When the specimen is clearly seen, use the fine adjustment to get it in perfect focus. *Never* reverse the procedure and focus downward, because you may break the slide, or worse, the objective.

When the specimen is in perfect focus under low power, you are now ready to switch to the high power. Slowly swing the high power objective into line with the body tube. The objective looks as though it will strike the slide, but it will not if the objectives are parfocal and the slide is not unusually thick. Keep moving the objective until you hear a click. Change the diaphragm opening to admit more light. Look through the eyepiece and carefully get the specimen in focus, using the fine adjustment. Coarse adjustment isn't used with high magnification objectives.

Learn to keep both eyes open while looking through the eyepiece. It is very tiring to hold one eye open and the other closed for long periods of time. If you keep both eyes open from the very start, you'll learn to ignore what the eye not looking through the eyepiece is seeing. Use one eye for a half hour, then switch to the other for the next half hour. Don't be surprised if you find yourself squinting with one eye closed. Just open your eyes and keep looking.

Before we examine moving specimens in pond water, let's practice with an imprint of the underside of a leaf from a household plant. A spider plant leaf or African violet leaf is an excellent choice, but any plant leaf will do. You will also need a plastic coverslip and a small amount of acetone. If you don't have any acetone, use your mother's nail polish remover—it contains acetone. The acetone will soften the coverslip enough that it will make an imprint of the leaf. First clean the coverslip with lens paper, then lay it on a tabletop that has been covered with a piece of newspaper. Place a small drop of acetone in the center of the coverslip and quickly place the leaf with its underside down on top of the drop. Hold the leaf firmly in place with your thumb for one minute without moving. After a minute, remove the leaf. Examine the coverslip. Looking closely, you should see some fine, etched lines that are a permanent imprint of the underside of the leaf. Mount the coverslip on the stage, and get it in focus with the low power objective. You should see an imprint of the cells, tiny veins and stomates (microscopic openings). You may see some hairs. Switch to the high power objective and notice how much bigger things are. Since the field of view is smaller and the light dimmer (see *Figures 12a–d*), adjust the light so you can see the image better.

Millions of years ago, leaves fell from prehistoric trees onto soft mud and were covered and held firmly in place. When the mud hardened into rock, the imprint of the leaves remained in the rock and can be seen to this day. Preserved microscopic fossils of 3.5 billion-year-old algae have also been discovered. Further along in this book we will tell how you can observe pieces of rock under the microscope, including those with preserved fossil imprints.

One question that often arises for the microscope hunter is "How big is that cell?" Professionals use costly micrometers to accurately measure what they see with the microscope. But we will be using a cheaper device that will suffice for our purposes: a clear plastic ruler.

Mount a clear plastic ruler on the stage so that the edge of the millimeter scale is across the center of the field. Notice how thick the millimeter lines appear under low power. Move the ruler until the center of one line is just visible at the left side of the field (see *Figure 13*). The distance to the center of the next line is 1 mm. or 1,000 microns. Count the number of millimeter lines you can see. Probably a millimeter line will not be visible at the right edge of the field. You will just have to estimate how much of the millimeter is left over on the right side. *Figure 13* shows the field to measure about 1.9 millimeters (or about 1,900 microns at 100X). When we switch to high power, we

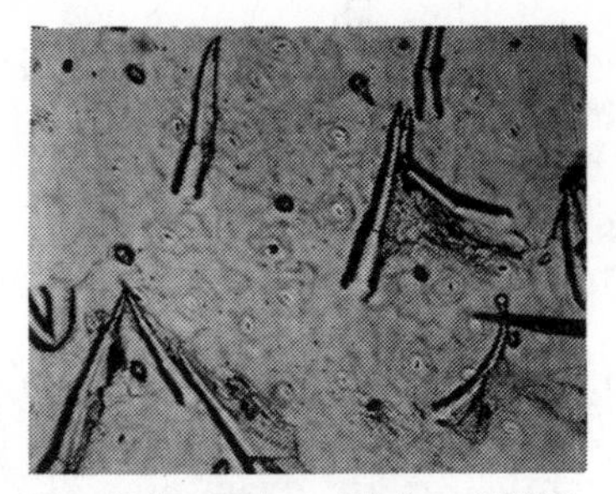

Fig. 12A. African Violet (100X)

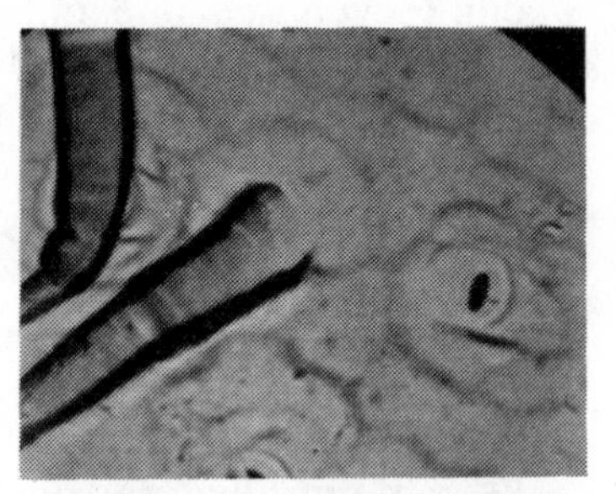

Fig. 12B. African Violet (400X)

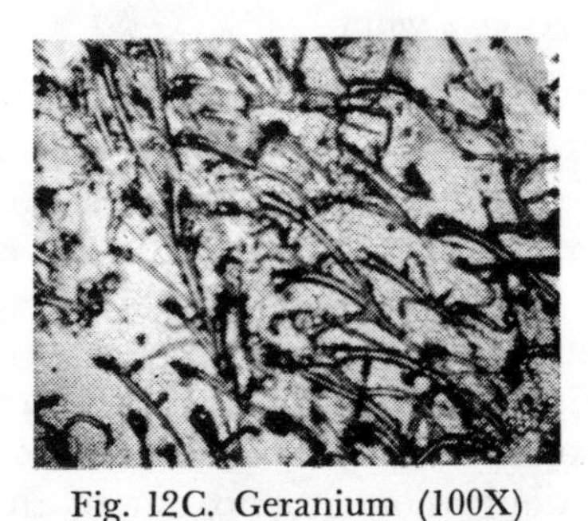

Fig. 12C. Geranium (100X)

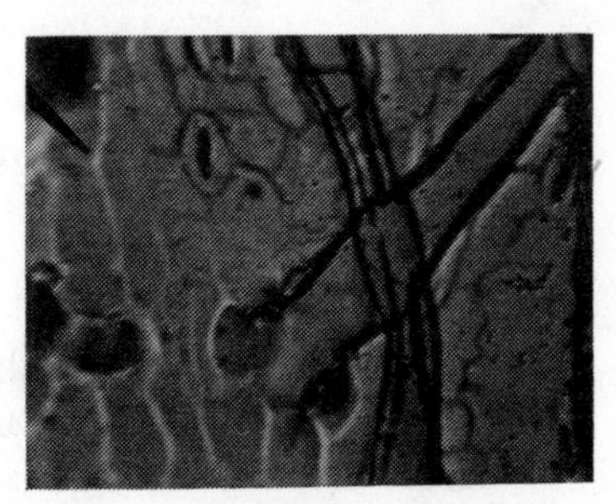

Fig. 12D. Geranium (400X)

Fig. 12. Comparison of possible magnifications

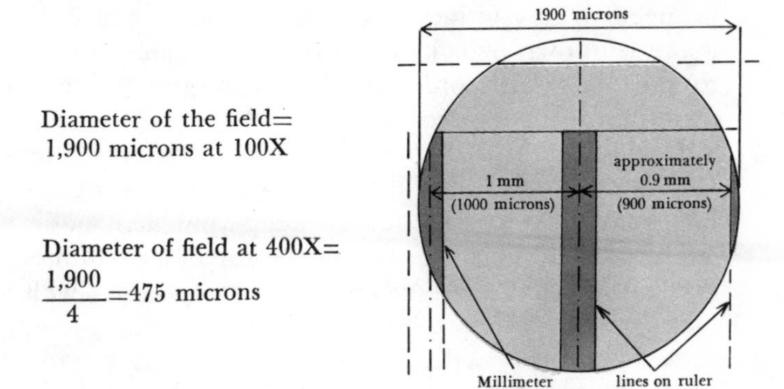

Fig. 13. How to measure with the microscope.

don't even see one millimeter line. However, since the field of view at 400X will be one-fourth that seen at 100X, we can estimate the diameter of the field of view under high power. In this case it will be 475 microns—1,900 microns divided by 4 equals 475 microns. Practice estimating the size of the leaf structure, using the imprint you made previously.

Since we are planning to "bring back alive" the strange wild animals we capture in the pond, we must learn how to keep them alive and well while we are examining them under the lens of our instrument.

HOW TO MAKE AND USE A WELL SLIDE

If we place a drop or two of water containing microscopic animals on a glass slide and put a cover glass over it, the weight of the cover glass is sufficient to crush and ruin many of the interesting creatures in the drop of water. Therefore, we must provide some sort of a miniature pond in which they can swim about freely.

This is easily done by using a *well slide* (see *Figure 14*). Dealers in microscopic supplies sell two kinds of well slides, one with a shallow depression ground out of the slide itself, and the other with vertical walls forming a well. The latter is better but more expensive. However, there is no need to buy either kind ready-made as you can easily make your own by cementing pierced squares of cardboard to the slide with ordinary shellac as glue. The shellac waterproofs the cardboard.

If you work in a warm room you will notice that the water rapidly evaporates around the edges of the cover glass, killing your little menagerie. To keep your menagerie well-supplied with moisture, cut off the top of a small medicine vial and cement the bottom to a corner of your well slide (see *Figure 14*). Lay a bit of cotton wick across the edge of the cover glass with the other end hanging into the medicine vial which you have filled with water. Without any attention from you, the water from the tiny reservoir is

FIG. 14
WELL - SLIDES AND DIPPING TUBE
Cut-off vial
Well-slide with Depression ground in glass.
Well-slide with wick and reservoir to keep well full.
Cardboard soaked in shellac
Stick square on slip with shellac to make well
How to keep water in well-slide with wick in drinking glass or cup.
Using dipping tube to removed water from collecting jar.

carried along the cotton wick to the edge of the cover glass to replace the water lost by evaporation.

HOW TO KEEP SPECIMENS OVERNIGHT

Sooner or later in your hunting adventures you are sure to come across some specimen so beautiful that you will want to keep it for study the following day, or to show someone else who wasn't there when the discovery was made.

If you return the water containing the wonderful specimen from the well slide to the aquarium or pond-water bottle, it will be lost. What to do?

One of the sketches in *Figure 14* shows the simple procedure that will enable you to set the well slide aside and keep your specimen in good condition for several days. Lay the covered well slide across a water glass or cup filled with water and lay a bit of cotton wick across the edge of the cover glass with both ends of the wick hanging into the water below. Capillary action in the wick will continuously draw up fresh water for the tiny creatures, and supply it to the specimen under the cover glass.

HOW TO USE A DIPPING TUBE

Another simple device that you will find indispensable is the *dipping tube.* This is just a medicine dropper with the bulb removed. *Figure* 14 shows how to use it. Place the forefinger firmly over the top of the tube and plunge the lower end into the water of the aquarium or pond-water bottle. Then, as you remove your finger, some of the water will rush into the tube. When this occurs, replace your finger on the upper opening. You can transfer the water to a well slide by releasing the finger from the upper end of the dipping tube.

Sometimes you may want to capture a small "water flea" or some other creature just visible to your eye. For closer observation as he moves about in the aquarium, use the dipping tube as described above. However, after plunging the dipping tube into the water, follow the creature's movement with the lower end of the tube, keeping the opening directly above him. Then suddenly remove your finger from the upper end, and as the water rushes in, the water flea may be carried along. If he isn't, try again. After you have captured him, transfer him to a well slide for observation.

When you observe live creatures, notice that they frequently move out of the field you are observing through the microscope. To follow them you must become expert in moving the slide about on the microscope stage without removing your eye from the eyepiece. This may be confusing at first because the field moves opposite to the direction you move the slide. If you move the slide left, the viewing field appears to move right and vice-versa.

FIELD OBSERVATIONS WITH A WELL SLIDE

If you like to hike you can have a lot of fun in summer by taking a well slide, cover glasses, a dipping tube and a ten- or twelve-diameter pocket magnifying lens. Transfer a few drops of water from what appears to be a promising spot among the weeds alongside the pond shore to your well slide, place cover glass over the well, and examine with your pocket lens. You can see many of the larger creatures and, in time, you will learn to detect the presence of creatures as small as *Vorticellae*. When you do this, wash off the water containing them into your collecting bottle so you may recapture and study them later.

COVERS, SLIDES, BALSAM

Little need be said about the regular flat glass slides and thin cover glass, for every optical supply store that sells microscopes also supplies these accessories. You will find, however, especially for observing live creatures in the well slide, that the one-inch square cover glasses are the most convenient and easily handled. Microscope dealers also carry small jars of *Canada Balsam*, a sticky resinous liquid that microscopists use for mounting objects permanently on slides.

HOW TO MOUNT IN BALSAM

To mount any small dry object (such as a fly's wing), simply place the object in the center of a glass slide and let a drop of Canada Balsam fall upon it. Then place a clean cover slip upon the drop and press down very gently until the balsam spreads out to the edges of the cover glass. In a few days the balsam will be hard and the slide can be labelled and kept indefinitely.

HOW TO DEHYDRATE SPECIMENS

Do not try to mount in this way any object that contains water (such as a fly's tongue), for it will quickly dry up and spoil. Objects containing water must first be dehydrated (have their water removed) by soaking in successively more alcoholic mixtures of alcohol and water, and finally pure alcohol. This will remove all the water. Then soak the object in turpentine to increase its transparency. Finally, mount the object in Canada Balsam as described above. A mount prepared in this way will remain unchanged.

In dehydrating, begin with a mix of 30% alcohol (10 ml. alcohol to 20 ml. water). Leave the specimen in this solution five minutes, then transfer to 50% alcohol, then a 70% mixture, a 90% mixture, and finally a 100% alcohol solution, each time leaving the object in the solution for five minutes. By having several small bottles you can use the same solutions of alcohol over and over, though eventually they will be weakened by the water extracted from your specimens.

HOW TO MAKE A SCOOP NET

For collecting aquatic specimens, you will often find it convenient to purchase a fine mesh nylon net from a tropical fish store. These nets are quite cheap but very useful for scooping up floating water plants or for catching swimming insects. They have many uses.

When the net has hauled in its catch of weeds or objects, it can be held over the wide mouth collecting bottle and turned inside out into the water in the bottle.

Now we have finished with the necessary technical advice and are ready for the really fascinating part of the microscopic work—the actual finding and identification of the microscopic plants and animals. The pictures in the following chapters show the varieties that will most frequently be found by hunters in the micro-jungle of the pond.

IV

WHERE AND HOW TO HUNT MICROSCOPIC BIG GAME

Many a person has failed to find the pleasure that there is in the possession of a good microscope simply because he, or she, lacked a few simple directions about where to secure a supply of constantly new and really interesting objects for observation.

All too frequently somebody, fascinated by advertising which offers a microscope as the gateway to a world of wonder, blindly buys an instrument, with perhaps a few prepared "slides" of various objects. He looks with natural curiosity at the "tongue of a fly," the "foot of a spider," the "sting of a bee," and perhaps a "section of cornstalk." But he cannot go on looking at these indefinitely—especially as he is not helped in any way to understand what he is seeing. Accordingly, after a few days, the novelty of the new toy is worn off and it is put away, to be eventually sold or forgotten.

How different the story might be if every person who comes into possession of a fairly good microscope could learn at the start that a little vegetable matter from the bank of the nearest pond will furnish an inexhaustible wealth of fascinating *live* objects! Then, instead of discarding the microscope as devoid of interest after his first curiosity was satisfied, he would go on and develop it into a fascinating and perhaps life-long recreation.

And in few other recreations is the first cost almost the only cost, for the ponds or swamps are ready to furnish the microscope hobbyist, once he finds himself with a good instrument, with constantly new and endlessly interesting specimens for the mere trouble of going out and floating a little green vegetable matter into a wide-mouthed bottle, along with some of the surrounding water. Even a teaspoonful of it may furnish a delightful menagerie, large and varied enough to keep one pleasurably amazed for a whole week of evenings.

To furnish a complete guide to all the creatures which may be found in one summer's leisure-time examination of pond water is infinitely beyond the scope of this small book. At the end, a few other books will be mentioned which will enable you to go farther with the subject. In this book I can only mention briefly a few of the most frequently found microscopic creatures, and give you pictures which will enable you to recognize them when they appear under your microscope's objective.

But first it is necessary to point out the most likely hunting grounds where the microscopic pond creatures can be captured—the pastures where they graze most frequently.

To begin with, there is no more likely jungle for the microscopic hunter than a little of the tangled mass of hair-like green filaments which you will find floating loosely in the water at the edge of almost any summer pond. It may look almost repulsive—like slime in fact—but it is really a most clean and beautiful plant. You will agree when you have seen it under the microscope. Accordingly, loosen a little of it with your fingers, while the mass is still floating in the pond, and slip it over the tip of a small wide-mouthed bottle, letting water follow until the bottle is half-full. You should avoid lifting the green filaments *out* of the water before putting into the bottle, for many of your most desirable microscopic specimens may thus be dripped off with the water.

In addition to these green filamentous plants, called *Algae* or *Confervae,* there are a number of other larger varieties of water plants which frequently shelter quantities of the microscopic animals we are hunting.

A few of the most common of these plants are drawn simply in *Figure 15*. In collecting them the same precaution given for *Confervae* should be observed: namely, to float parts of the plants directly into your collecting bottle without lifting them clear of the water.

Most of these aquatic plants have narrow, finely divided leaves, between which it is easy for our extremely small prey to shelter themselves. Find any of the following plants and you will be practically sure to find interesting and greatly varied living objects for your microscope. But it will always be a lottery: you may find a beautiful specimen of a certain creature one day and then not see another for a long time. You may find great numbers of the same kind, or scarcely any two alike. This constant surprise of discovery is what makes pond water jungle-hunting such fun.

Now for a few comments upon the pictures in *Figure 15*, which will enable you to identify the principal pond plants. In doing this, float a single leaf of the plant in a white butterdish, and compare it with the pictures in *Figure 15*.

Do not let the scientific names "stump" you. It is much better to learn the correct titles at once, as some of them have no popular names. Besides, if you know the scientific name, every other micro-hobbyist will know at once what you mean. Botanists give much thought to finding a name which belongs exactly to a given species and no other, so why not use it? To use the correct scientific terms for everything connected with your hobby is a mark of efficiency and an orderly mind.

RANUNCULUS AQUATILIS

(*A* in *Figure 15*.) This plant grows under water in ponds and slow streams. The leaves, which divide

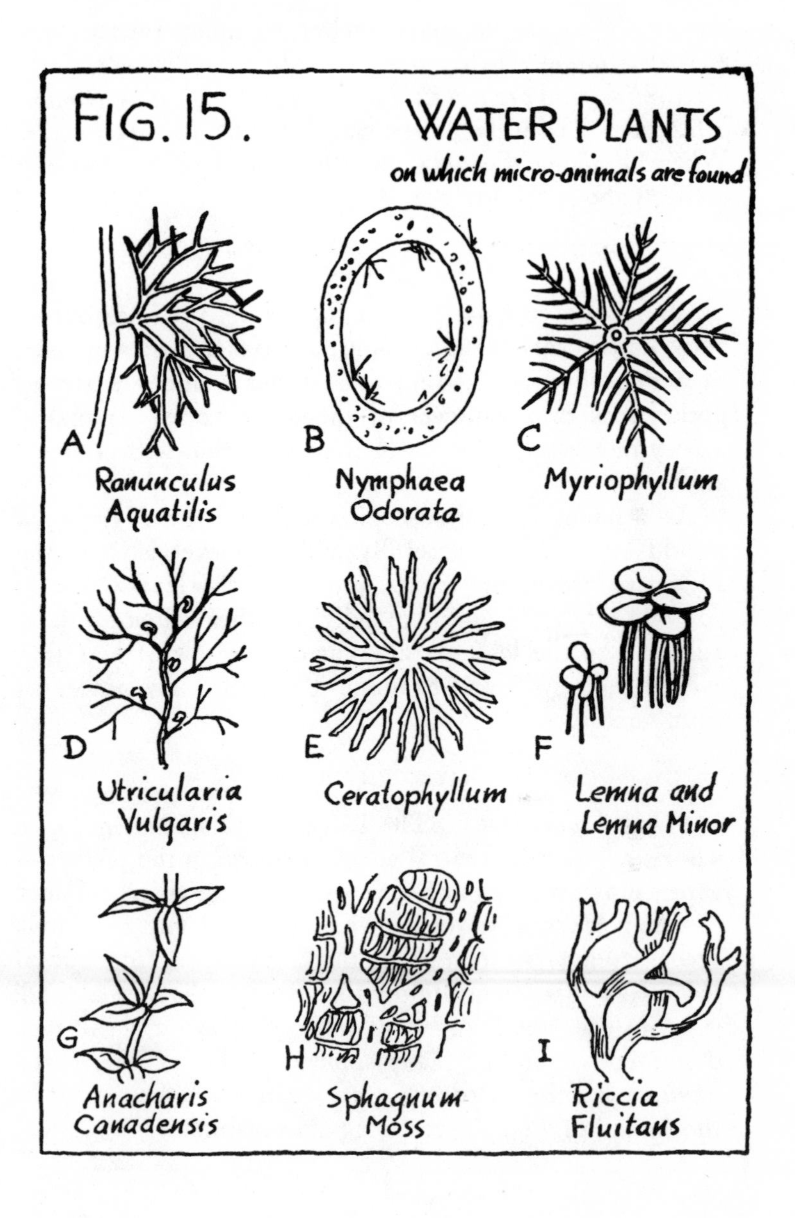

FIG. 15.
WATER PLANTS
on which micro-animals are found
A
Ranunculus Aquatilis
B
Nymphaea Odorata
C
Myriophyllum
D
Utricularia Vulgaris
E
Ceratophyllum
F
Lemna and Lemna Minor
G
Anacharis Canadensis
H
Sphagnum Moss
I
Riccia Fluitans

repeatedly as shown, offer shelter to many microscopic animals, among which you are most likely to find *Rotifers*, *Vorticellas*, and *Stentors*. (See Chapter 5.) The *Ranunculus* grows entirely under water except for its flower. When blooming, a single white blossom like a butter-cup is lifted above the surface.

NYMPHAEA ODORATA

White Water Lily. (*B* in *Figure 15.*) Since everybody knows this plant at sight, I have drawn a picture of a thin slice of its stem as it appears under a strong pocket lens or low-power of the microscope. It makes a very interesting object when cut very thin with a sharp knife.

As a haunt for microscopic creatures, the *Nymphaea* should be examined carefully with a pocket lens on the under surface of the leaves and along the leaf-stem. If you find any little lumps of jelly or other minute objects adhering to the leaf surface, cut out the bit of leaf that carries the object and examine it under a low power of your microscope.

MYRIOPHYLLUM

(*C* in *Figure 15.*) The leaves of this plant grow in whorls around the central stem, as shown in the picture—which shows a section of stem with a single whorl. When you find *Myriophyllum* growing, you will find it in long green streamers, round and thick. When lifted out of the water they seem almost like ropes. Cut off a small piece in the water and float into your bottle as already described. Another plant somewhat similar to *Myriophyllum* is called *Proserpinaca*. Either of these may be the haunt of many interesting micro-animals.

UTRICULARIA VULGARIS

(*D* in *Figure 15.*) This water plant is easily known by the presence of the little seed-like bladders, which give it its popular name, "Bladder-wort." These bladders are actually "stomachs," in which small water creatures are trapped and digested by the plant. The microscope hunter's main interest is, however, in the tiny organisms which may frequently be found clinging between its finely divided leaves. Clip off a small portion of one of these and place under a low-power objective.

CERATOPHYLLUM DEMERSUM

(*E* in *Figure 15.*) At first glance you may mistake this plant for *Myriophyllum,* but the likeness will no longer fool you if you cut off a single whorl and compare it with the pictures. You will then see that *Ceratophyllum* is coarser-leaved and rather stiff. Its name, in fact, means "horny-leaved." Also, little spines appear along the leaves. In examining it for possible creatures, cut off only a small piece and put in a "well-slide" filled with water. This plant is found in thick masses, in quiet shallow places in ponds or slow streams.

LEMNA POLYRRHIZA AND LEMNA MINOR

(*F* in *Figure 15.*) The rather silly popular name for this beautiful little floating plant is "duck-weed." It means nothing, as ducks do not eat it, or have anything to do with it. Each plant of *Lemna Polyrrhiza* is made up of little roundish green fronds as shown in the picture. The under-surfaces are a dull purple in color and from them several little white rootlets hang down into the water. The whole plant is hardly over a quarter of an inch across, but in summer large ponds are often covered with them, as with a carpet. Snip off a bit of one of the rootlets, and examine it in a well-slide under your microscope. You may be rewarded with sight of some fine *Vorticellas,* or perhaps *Hydras,* which are fond of perching there too. It is also a good hunting ground for finding *Rotifers.*

Lemna Minor is similar, except that the leaf-fronds are more oval and smaller. Also, their under surfaces are not purple, and have only one rootlet to each frond. Look for the same kind of creatures as on the larger *Lemna.*

ANACHARIS CANADENSIS

(*G* in *Figure 15.*) This plant grows under water, in long stems, which are surrounded by whorls of three leaves each, as shown in the picture. The leaves and stems are semi-transparent and rather tender, breaking easily. The spaces between the leaves are frequently shelters for many *Hydras,* but almost any other micro-animals may be found there too.

SPHAGNUM MOSS

(*H* in *Figure 15*) In this picture (as in *B* also) a magnified section is shown, rather than the complete plant. Note the water-holding spaces between the cells of the plant. The ability of this moss to hold water makes it very useful to florists who use it to pack live plants for shipment. The moss grows on the wet shores of shady bogs and swamps. Its principal interest for the microscope hobbyist is that it may be covered with *Infusoria, Rhizopoda, Diatoms* and *Desmids,* which will wash off in the water when a bit of moss is put in a well-slide and examined under the objective.

RICCIA FLUITANS

(*I* in *Figure 15.*) This plant grows in paper-thin green ribbons, sometimes an inch or more wide. It grows in long, branching strands, without roots, floating in the water. Like the other plants in this chapter, a bit of the leaf should be snipped off, put in a well-slide, and examined for any creatures which may be attached to it.

These few plants are the principal sources of micro-animals to be encountered in ponds and slow streams, but almost any bit of water vegetation is worth putting to the test of the microscope. You never know when even a two-millimeter sample of a green water plant may present you with some unsuspected marvel of the miniature world.

V

WHAT TO LOOK FOR WITH THE MICROSCOPE

THE SMALLER PLANTS OF THE MICRO-JUNGLE

When you enter the domain of the infinitely small in the water world, it becomes extremely difficult to tell plants from animals. In fact, over some of its denizens the scientific battle has raged for years. Plant? Or animal? And it is not surprising, for in the microscopic jungle some of the smaller plants move about looking for food quite as freely as do the animals.

PLANTS ARE GREEN—BUT NOT ALWAYS

However, there is one test that holds in the water world just as well as it does on dry land. On our walks in the fields and woods we generally feel fairly safe in identifying plants by their green color, and this is also a reasonably certain identifying feature in two of the three classes of tiny plants which appear in the fields of our microscope.

In this and the succeeding chapters we are going to follow the same plan that we did in the chapter on the subjects for the pocket lens: supply you with many pictures to help you recognize and name what you see, and make passing comments on those objects about which we know interesting little bits of gossip.

The three chief classes of microscopic plants are called *Algae, Desmids,* and *Diatoms.* The *Algae* and *Desmids* always show the green plant coloring-matter which we call "chlorophyl," but the *Diatoms* are apt to be as brown as the mud where they are frequently found.

A FEW OF THE "ALGAE"

(*Figure 16.*) The masses of long, stringy, green

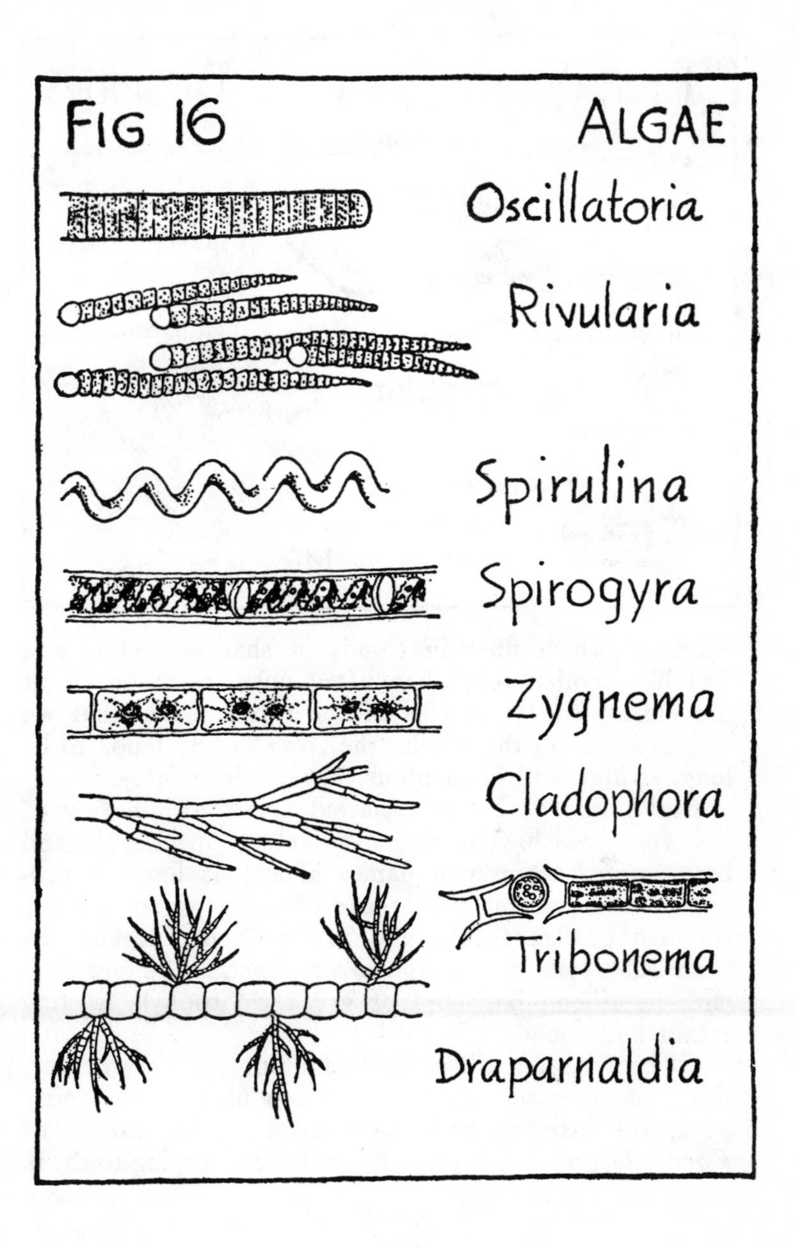
Fig 16
Algae
Oscillatoria
Rivularia
Spirulina
Spirogyra
Zygnema
Cladophora
Tribonema
Draparnaldia

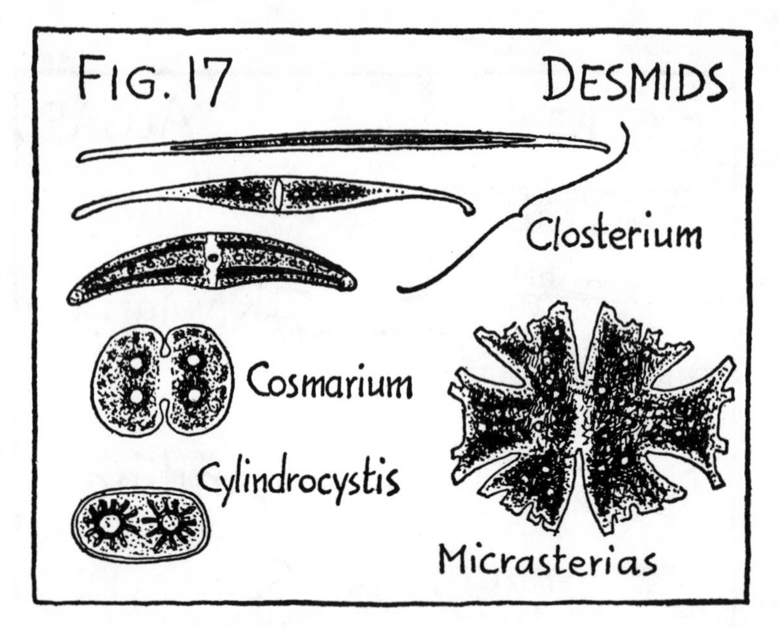

filaments which float in clouds in shallow water, and feel like sodden felt when lifted out, are made up of the most plentiful species of the water plants that we call *Algae.* On the whole, the *Alga* family tends to be long, stringy and filamentous, but not invariably.

In *Figure 16,* I have selected and drawn a few of the *Algae* which you are most likely to meet with, and have tagged them with names almost as hard to pronounce and remember as those of some of our equally common garden shrubs and plants. You will find the beautiful form called *Spirogyra* especially interesting, with its ribbon-like band of green chlorophyll twisting round and round.

Of course, you will never find a single variety of anything, plant or animal, alone. A few filaments of *Spirogyra,* for instance, may have lovely little colonies of *Vorticellae,* or Bell Flower Animalcules, hanging to them,

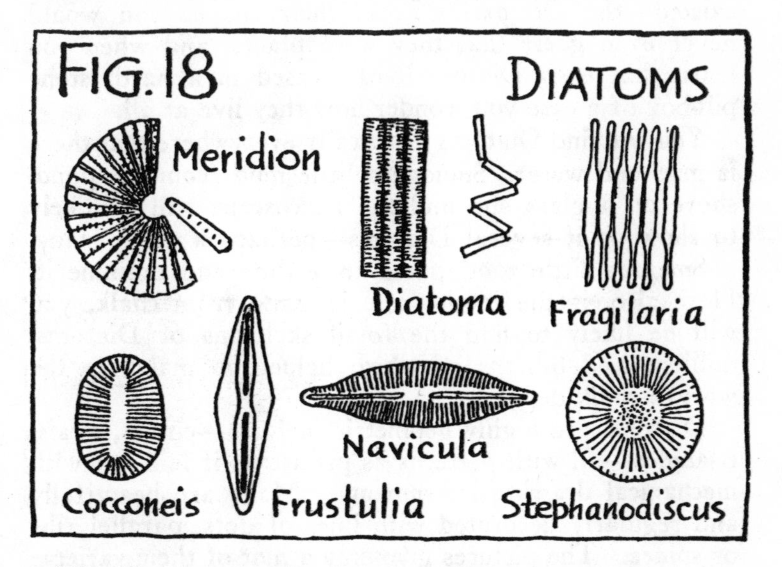

while all around swim *Rotifers, Volvox* and other creatures—a veritable menagerie. However, the only way we can show you what the individual plants and animals look like is to exhibit them in our pictures as they never are in real life—namely, classified. This book has to make a few concessions to systematic science.

THE SYMMETRICAL DESMIDS

(*Figure 17.*) While the members of the *Alga* family tend to form long strings of cells, the beautiful green *Desmids* are all single-celled. They tend to appear in balanced halves. These microscopic plants generally adhere to the stems and leaves of larger water plants, such as those described in Chapter 3.

THE HARD-SHELLED DIATOMS

(*Figure 18.*) These pictures represent a very few of one of the strangest families of plants that ever existed—the *Diatoms.* From their shapes you would never even guess that they were plants, and when you learn that each Diatom lives incased in a hard, stone pill-box of a case you wonder how they live at all.

You will find Diatoms practically everywhere that there is mud and water. Smudge a little mud from the pond-shore on a glass slip and the microscope will be likely to show on it several Diatoms—perhaps a great many.

Smear a little tooth paste on a slide and examine it. Here also, if the tooth paste is made from chalk, you will be likely to find the fossil skeletons of Diatoms, millions and billions of which helped to make up the world's chalk deposits.

Diatoms are highly geometric in form—circles, ovals, triangles—all with patterns as precise as if laid out with mechanical drawing instruments. Many are beautifully and regularly decorated with lines of dots, parallel ribs or spines. The pictures give only a hint of their variety: there are over 1,200 species.

Animals with Roots for Feet and with Whips for Propellers—and a Garden of Flower-Animals

AMOEBA AND ITS COUSINS

If, when looking through your microscope at water life, you see what looks like a tiny dab of colorless jelly, watch it for a moment or two. It may extend a part of its main body into a rather shapeless arm or leg, (call it a "root" if you like) which may eventually be drawn back into the body again. If you see this happen, you will probably be watching an *amoeba*—the simplest member of the family which have been named the "rhizopods," or the "root-footed" creatures. (From *rhizo,* "root" and *pod,* "foot." The amoeba and its relatives are simple one-celled creatures that are probably quite similar to the first living animals that developed on the earth more than one billion years ago. Amoeba are usually found on the

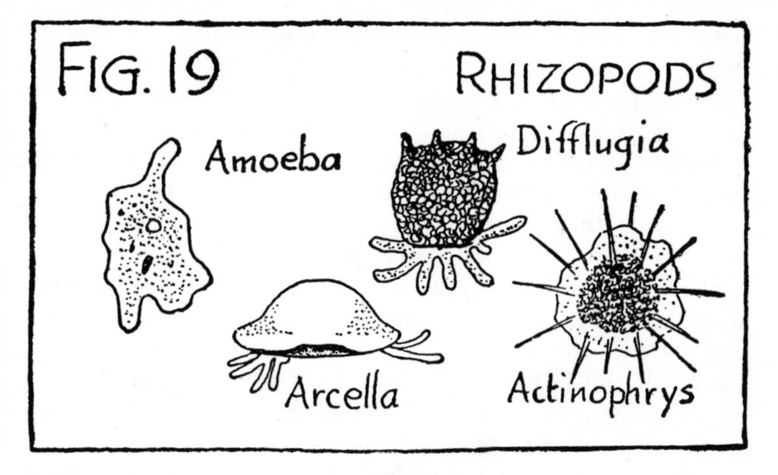

underside of water-lily pads or on the stems of water plants. If you carefully transfer some of the slimy material from there to a slide, and cover it with a cover glass, you may see the grayish, granular, jelly-like mass that makes up the amoeba. It moves by flowing into its extensions or *pseudopods* (false feet). It has no particular shape, since it is always moving in this way (see *Figure 19*). If the amoeba comes in contact with a food particle as it moves about, it simply flows around it. It eats by engulfing food particles. The food is then digested inside of the amoeba. Under a low power microscope look for small dense portions inside the amoeba that are larger than the tiniest granules; these are the places where the food is being digested.

To grow amoebas you will need pure water (preferably filtered pond water or aquarium water) and a small glass container; you can even use a shot glass. The quality of the water is most important since these tiny animals are easily poisoned by metallic impurities from water pipes, such as lead or copper.

While amoebas may not be fussy eaters, you mustn't overfeed them. If you do, bacteria will foul the water and the amoeba and its relatives will die. Try experimenting with different kinds and quantities of foods. You might make an important discovery!

One way to grow food for your amoebas is to dry a small quantity of lettuce in your oven until it is crisp. Boil 50 ml. of water and add about 0.5 gr. of the dried lettuce. Let this food mixture stand for two or three days, then add your amoebas with your medicine dropper. Rotifers and many other kinds of animals will also grow in this mixture. From time to time, add a dropper full of water. The depth of the water should not be more than two centimeters. Be sure air can get into the container. As the amoebas become abundant, stir the liquid and pour half of it into another container prepared the same way. This should be done every six weeks. Another food mixture can be made by adding one drop of skim milk and two boiled rice grains to the boiled water instead of lettuce. The mixture will cloud, indicating that bacteria, the food your microscopic animals feed on, are present.

INVENTORS OF THE "PULL" PROPELLER

Someday you may notice in the water under your objective a little green ball, apparently containing a few smaller ones. The green ball rolls along through the water with no apparent cause. However, if you get the quantity and direction of your light source arranged just right, you will see that the sphere is propelled by the lashing of many tiny thread-like whips.

You are looking at a Volvox, one of the group of microscopic creatures called the *Flagellates*, or *whip-bearers*. These creatures have many extraordinary shapes, as you will see from the sketches in *Figure 20*, but all are related in one way—they propel themselves through the water by lashing their whip-like flagellae. Though the picture this brings to mind is a creature propelled by lashing out behind itself with its whip, usually you will find that the lash is vibrated ahead of the organism which is pulled after its whip, just as an airplane is driven by being pulled after its propeller.

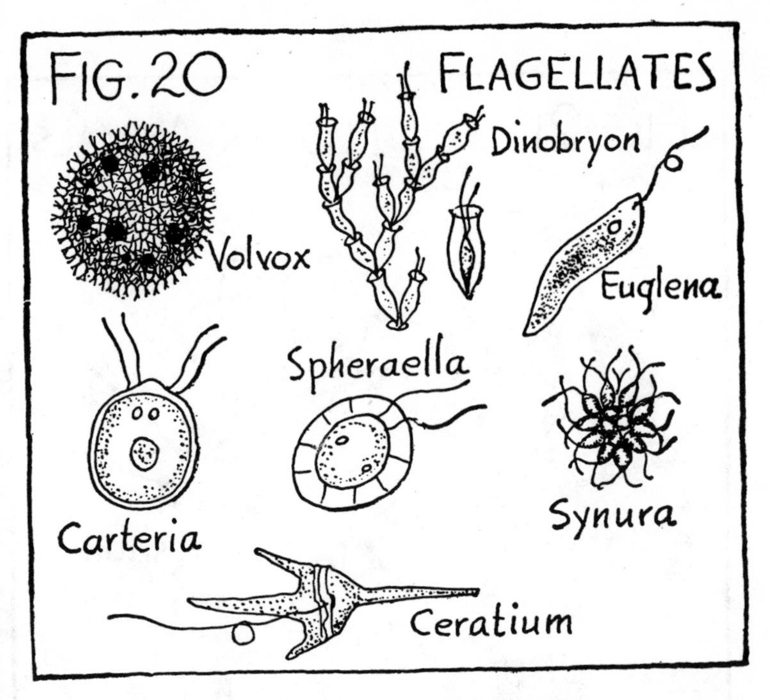

WHEN ANIMALS BECOME BLOSSOMS

Until you have seen a colony of *Vorticellae* (or Bell-flower Animalcules) you do not know what fascination your microscope is capable of delivering. When you catch sight of them, you will instantly think of a bed of infinitesimal tulips, apparently attached to and growing out of a thread of green algae. But as you watch, you will be amazed to see the stem of a first one "tulip," and then another and another suddenly shorten and its blossom drop to the bottom. It happens so quickly that, at first, you don't know where to look for the blossoms. It is only when you see them slowly rising up again as their stems straighten out from the "spiral spring" shape into which they have suddenly contracted, that you realize where the "blossoms" went when they vanished.

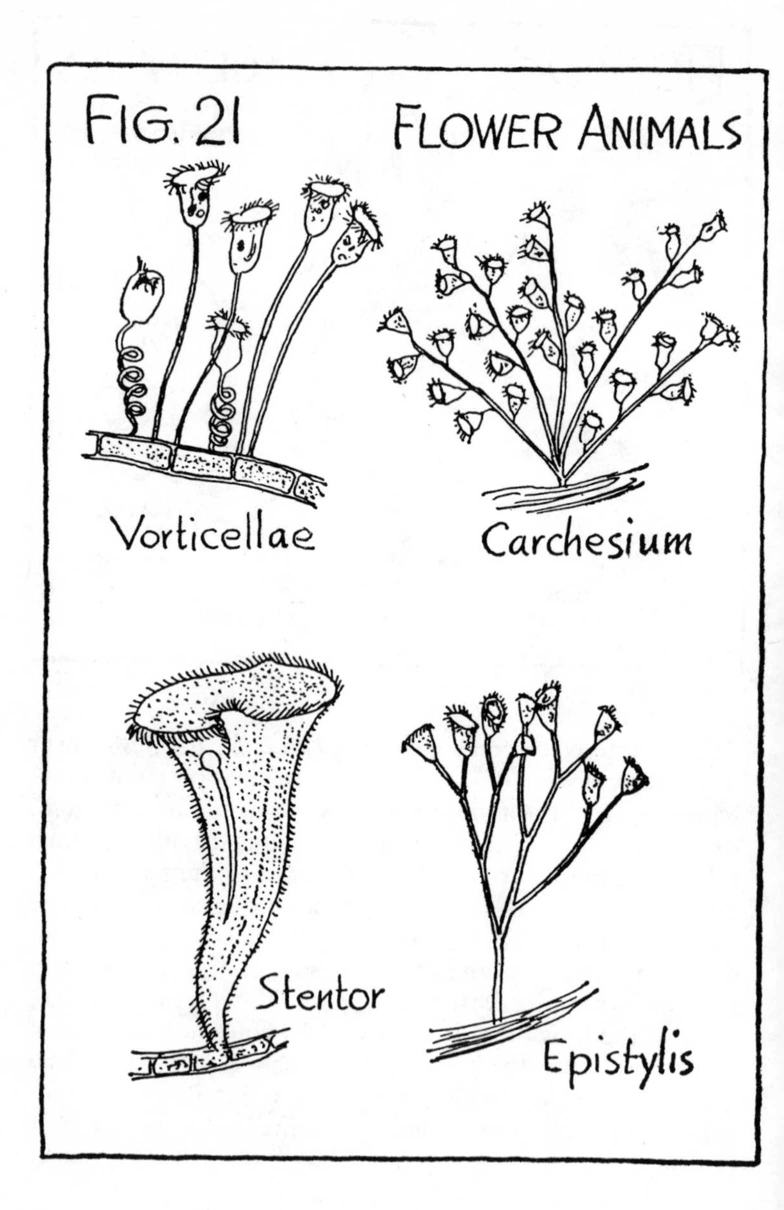
FIG. 21
FLOWER ANIMALS
Vorticellae
Carchesium
Stentor
Epistylis

Along with the *Vorticellae* in *Figure 21*, other kinds of flower animals are pictured including the *Stentor. This flower* animal looks more like a horn or a trumpet, and this is what its name means. *Stentor,* too, may be found attached to a piece of algae or duckweed, but they often can be seen swimming about near the surface of the pond or the water in your collecting jar. You might be able to see a *Stentor* without a hand lens or microscope because one species measures about two millimeters and is bluish in color. *Stentor* feed on smaller one-celled animals in the pond and, in turn, is food for larger animals.

A CARNIVOROUS PALM TREE

Another minute creature which you will frequently find attached to things by a stem, although it is decidedly an animal, and a carnivorous one at that, is the famous freshwater *Hydra*. It can be seen in *Figure 22*.

If you collect bottles of pond water frequently, you will probably find many *Hydras* sticking to the inside surface of the glass. The *Hydra* is fascinating in many ways. Its tentacles contain many stinging cells that paralyze any tiny creature unfortunate enough to swim against a tentacle. Even a baby fish, larger than the *Hydra,* can be captured and then swallowed by this remarkable pond dweller. One of its favorite foods is the *Daphnia* (see *page 72*). Watching a *Hydra* feed on these "water fleas" can be an exciting adventure. Pick up a Daphnia with a medicine dropper, place it close to the *Hydra,* then watch what happens.

Some *Hydras* are males while others are female, just like people; however, unlike people, they reproduce by budding. During the warm months of the year, healthy *Hydras* form buds on the walls of their tube-like bodies as shown in *Figure 22*. Each bud will grow, form tentacles, then pinch off to lead a life of its own. W. F. Loomis, an authority on *Hydras,* noticed that when the amount of carbon dioxide

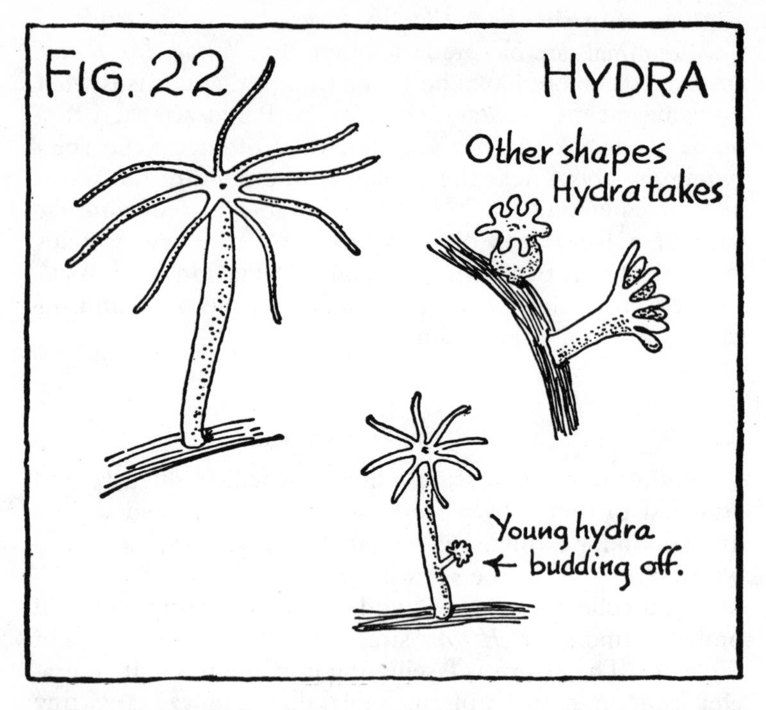

(CO_2) dissolved in their watery environment was higher than normal, the *Hydras* developed either male or female reproductive organs instead of buds. If you collect your specimens from stagnant water, you will stand a good chance of finding *Hydras* in this unusual state. It is possible to simulate stagnant water conditions in the *Hydras'* environment at home by using a jar with a small opening that holds a large volume of water, about a liter. Always keep the jar full so that the surface of the water will absorb very little oxygen (O_2). This will cause the CO_2 content of the water in the jar to increase.

There are several precautions necessary to raise *Hydra* successfully at home. Never use tap water, since dissolved copper from the pipes will surely kill your animals. Rain water you've collected in clean glass containers, pond water, or well water will do nicely. Another source of water is from an established aquarium. Avoid placing your *Hydras'* home in direct sunlight; room temperature and normal lighting are necessary. Feed them only live food such as Daphnia or Tubifex worms, both of which can either be bought in a pet shop or brought back from the wild. More about Daphnia on page 70.

ROTIFERS—THE MICRO-ANIMALS THAT EAT WITH A VENTILATING FAN

Figure 23 shows the recognizable portraits of a few of the remarkable family of microscopic creatures called *Rotifers* or *wheel-bearers*.

The early microscope pioneers discovered them in pond water, just as you will, and were so fascinated by the apparent rotation of the spokes of wheels around the mouths of the animals that no other name would do. They had to be named wheel bearers, and you will agree with the appropriateness of the name the moment you see a Rotifer's wheel rotating as he perches upon a thread of algae or swims through the microscopic swamp. To me, however, the motion always suggests the whirling of an electric fan, like those you see in the windows of restaurant kitchens to exhaust overheated air. This also expresses what is really happening in the Rotifer's case, for the motion creates a current in the water that sucks particles of food into the Rotifer's mouth. You know that it is food because the creature's body is transparent and you can see the peculiar "set of teeth" in its throat grinding away for dear life!

The Rotifer also uses its wheel to propel itself through the water, just as the rotating propeller of a motor boat moves it through the water.

I am sure that you are doubtful that a wheel can actually be revolving in a creature's mouth, so it may be well to explain that the apparent rotation is an optical illusion. The illusion is caused by the rapid bending down and recovering of a circular row of *cilia*—tiny hairs like your eyelashes. It is the same illusion that makes the border of an electric sign appear to move. The line of light seems to revolve around the sign, but the cause is many series of three or four bulbs in a row going on and off in rapid succession.

The Rotifers present so many fascinations that I am sure that they will quickly become the favorites in your micro-menagerie, entrancing you as they have generations of microscope hobbyists. One very startling feature of many Rotifers are their "telescopic tails." The sections actually slide into each other like the sections of a spyglass, thus enabling the creatures to fold themselves up into a shorter length.

Most Rotifers are so active that they give you good practice in moving the slide under the objective without removing your eye from the ocular. However, some members of this family are not swimmers at all; they live all their lives in tubular houses that they build and attach to water plants.

One of the most remarkable of these is shown in *Figure 23* over the amazingly girlish name of *Melicerta*. Melicerta is at once brickmaker, mason, and architect, building herself a chimney-like house out of little mudballs that she molds one by one before adding them to the circular wall.

The Melicerta's tubular homes are just large enough to be seen with the naked eye. With your pocket lens you can sometimes find them adhering in groups to the underside of a pond-lily leaf. In this case, clip out the bit of leaf carefully and put it into a well slide with water for observation under the pocket lens and microscope. Later, put the bit of leaf into a vial of water and keep the water fresh. In this way a specimen can be preserved alive for several days and transferred to the well slide when you want to exhibit your find to admiring friends. If you watch, you may even see Melicerta making bricks to lengthen her house.

So much for the Rotifer family. You will find them fascinating, from the very first glimpse you obtain of the commonest kind to your final delighted discovery of some of the rarest varieties.

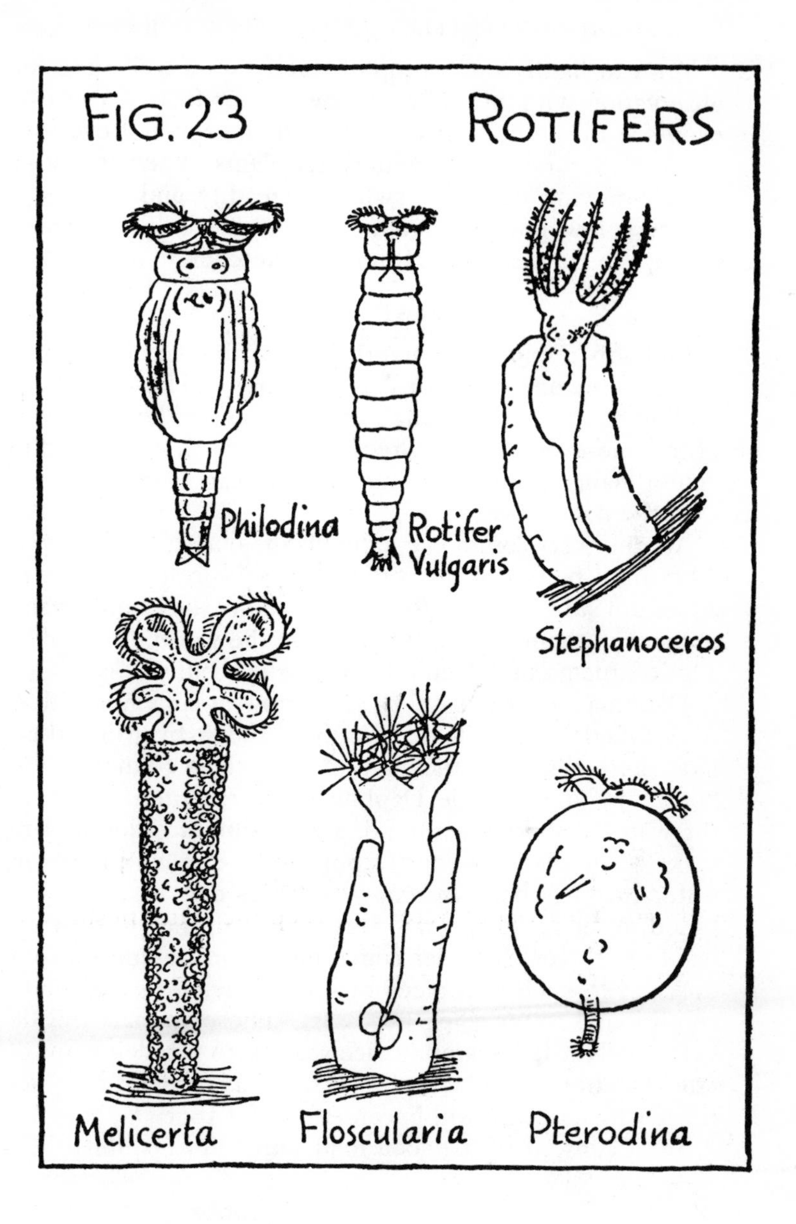
Fig. 23
Rotifers
Philodina
Rotifer Vulgaris
Stephanoceros
Melicerta
Floscularia
Pterodina

HUNTING WATER FLEAS AND DWELLERS IN JELLY

You can hardly put a drop of water into a well slide for observation without adding a few "water fleas." You can even see these little crustaceans with your naked eye in a bottle of water collected with water plants. They are those rapidly-moving dots that swim so steadily and tirelessly. Under a low power of your microscope you'll reçognize principal varieties easily from the sketches in *Figure 24*.

CYCLOPS IN MINIATURE

Probably the most frequently seen of all your microscopic quarry is the one called *Cyclops*, with her two little egg bags trailing behind and the single eye which gives her the name of the one-eyed giant of Greek mythology. It seems odd to give a giant's name to a creature that can hardly be seen with the naked eye!

Another very common creature is the one called *Daphnia*. The dried bodies of this variety are sold in little boxes in aquarium stores as food for goldfish. This shows how many millions of them are in every pond in the world, for it takes a lot of microscopic Daphnia to weigh an ounce.

Daphnia are easy to culture and grow in large quantities. Also called "water fleas," Daphnia move by using their large antennae like the oars of a rowboat. When these "oars" are stroked, the Daphnia seem to jump forward in the water. An old aquarium or a wide-mouth gallon jar will make a fine place for your Daphnia to live. You can use tap water that has been *conditioned*—water that has been exposed to the air for several days so that all the chlorine gas has left it. Cover the jar containing your Daphnia with a dust cover, such as a piece of glass plate. Be sure to add conditioned water when necessary. These animals will do very nicely if fed bacteria twice a week. A small amount of crushed, freshly boiled egg will serve as food for the bacteria, which in turn will become food for your Daphnia.

Yeast cells are also a good food source for Daphnia. Mix

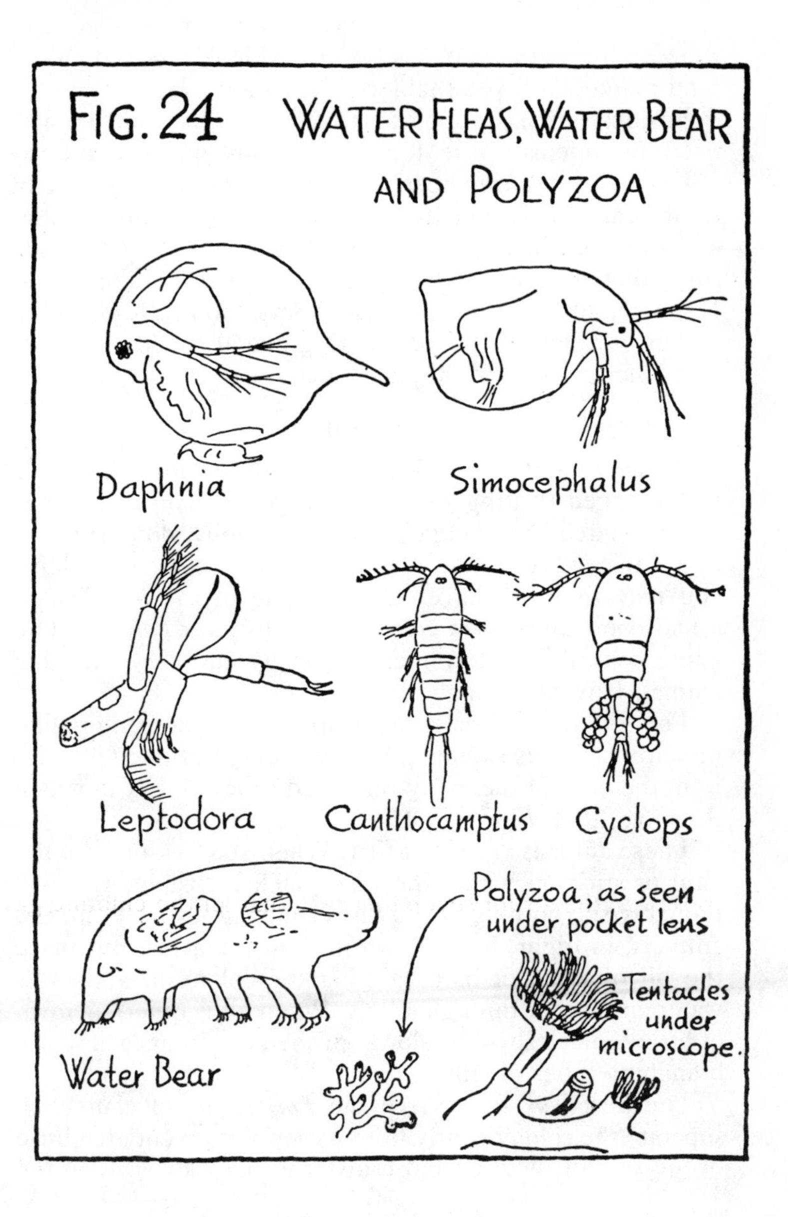

FIG. 24 WATER FLEAS, WATER BEAR AND POLYZOA

two grams of a compressed yeast tablet in five cubic centimeters of water that has been previously boiled. Most food markets sell yeast tablets in the dairy case.

Besides serving as food for the Hydra, Daphnia are also used by microscopists for many kinds of experiments. Their rapidly beating hearts are easily seen, and the rate of their heartbeat is quickly affected by drugs, temperature, and other factors. Their internal organs are easy to study since they are quite visible through their glass-like shells. Daphnia, like us, manufacture hemoglobin. Hemoglobin makes our blood red, and the Daphnia also take on a reddish color because of this substance.

POLYPS IN JELLY

If, when hunting pond material, you should turn over a water-logged floating stick or sodden chip and see a little mass or patch of shining clear or brown jelly, don't throw it away. Instead, examine it carefully with your pocket lens; you may find you have captured one of the loveliest of microscopic objects—a colony of fresh-water *Polyzoa.* The name comes from *poly* meaning many and *zoon* meaning animal. It is, accordingly, many animals.

The different animals composing a colony look more like miniature flowers as they protrude their petal-like tentacles from the ends of the many-branched tubes of jelly in which they live. (See *Figure 24.*)

These animals are shy at first. When you first pick up the chip or stick on which the jelly-patch is visible, you will probably see nothing of the flower-like appearance, for the animals, in fright, have drawn in their tentacles. But place the bit of wood or bark carrying the colony in a glass of water and watch through a lens. When all is quiet, a crown of little tentacles will be slowly pushed out from each of the branching tubes of jelly.

The best way to observe the *Polyzoa* is, of course, to separate the colony gently from its support (or cut off a little of the support with it) and transfer it to a water-cell on the microscopic stage. The tentacles (see *Figure 24*) are then a beautiful sight under a power of 50 or 60 diameters, especially if the light can be arranged to come obliquely from the side or can be cast from reading glass held above the water-cell.

Do not be surprised at the size of any colony of *Polyzoa* you may find, for occasionally one covers the entire underside of a waterlogged plank. The largest I ever heard of covered the entire circumference of an old wagon wheel that had been allowed to float indefinitely in a shady pond in the woods. However, you will find them more often as mere patches on chips, twigs, leaves, and so on.

VI

HOW TO DO MICROSCOPIC DETECTIVE WORK

One of the most fascinating fields you can enter with both your pocket lens and your microscope is the detection of crime! This doesn't mean that you can instantly start solving murder mysteries, but you can gradually become expert at identifying many everyday substances like coffee, cloth, flour, grains, spices, and so on. And, who knows, you might find microscopic detective work so exciting that you will gradually qualify as an expert in one of the branches that is really indispensable in crime detection.

This chapter contains the basics of several fields of identification that you can follow up, if you wish, with the aid of books on these specialties in forensics, or legal microscopy. The basics include fingerprint investigation and the study of forgeries in penmanship. Subjects like these, aside from their inherent interest, enable you to pursue your hobby at times when pond specimens, insects, and other nature material are scarce.

IDENTIFYING FIBERS

The appearances of cotton, silk, wool fibers, and synthetics such as nylon and polyester are so characteristic that, once you are familiar with them, you will be able to identify them under any circumstance.

To start, pull out threads of each of these materials from bits of cloth whose composition you know. Shred the threads apart with the points of large needles until you have the individual fibers separated. Then put a few of each kind on separate slides and become familiar with the appearance of cotton, linen, silk, wool, polyester, nylon, and any other man-made fibers that may come your way. View them both dry and mounted in water under a cover glass.

Figure 25 shows roughly what to expect in each case, but a few comments will help, and actual experience will soon make you an expert detector of these common materials.

Cotton Fiber has a flat and twisted appearance, as shown in the picture. The ribbon-like fiber appears to be thicker and rounded along the edges, and this appearance is explained when we learn that each fiber is really a long collapsed and twisted tube.

Linen Fiber is also a tube, but its walls are so thick that it does not collapse and become a flat ribbon. This clearly distinguishes it from cotton. In addition, you will notice that a linen fiber has frequent small swellings or knobs. The canal in the center is merely a narrow line in the middle of the fiber.

Silk Fiber is easy to differentiate from linen, because silk is solid like a thread of solid glass and its diameter is even throughout its length.

Wool Fiber is quite different in character from any of the other natural fibers, for it shows a broken or "scaly" appearance under the microscope.

Polyester Fiber looks granular, and its borders are not smooth or regular. Little lumps of material sticking out from the fibers cause larger masses to gather here in time. Soon they become visible and are called "pills" because of their shape.

Nylon Fiber looks very similar to silk under the microscope. Careful examination, however, will reveal that the nylon fiber is twisted into a spiral where silk fibers lie straight. You will see that nylon fibers tend to form loops very easily while silk fibers do not.

Some fabrics contain both natural and man-made fibers. These combinations are very interesting to examine microscopically. A very common combination shown in *Figure 25* is 65% polyester and 35% cotton. This means you should see almost twice as many polyester fibers as cotton.

If you have a companion in your microscopic researches, you can make a very interesting game of examining "mixed unknowns." In this procedure, a slide on which an unknown fiber sample (say 50% silk and 50% polyester) is placed in water under a cover glass by one person and handed to the other for identification. This is done, of course, after both of you have learned to identify the fabric fibers. By solving these unknowns, you will become more expert an investigator than in any other way. You can now determine the real content of a fabric that claims to be 100% wool. Just take a sample fiber and determine if the label is correct.

IDENTIFYING HAIRS

The importance of hair as evidence in criminal cases cannot be overstated. Using modern techniques, criminal investigators can tell if a hair is from a human or a particular animal species. If it is human, they can tell if it has been dyed or bleached, and even what part of the body it came from! One man was recently convicted of shooting a deer out of season on the evidence of deer hair found in the back of his brand-new truck.

Let's start with a human hair, from your own head if necessary. Prepare a wet mount by placing the hair on a clean slide, add a drop of water and then a cover glass.

The hair shaft has three main parts (see *Figure 26*). They are an inner *medulla* that appears black and irregular in *Figure 26*, surrounded by the main hollow shaft called the *cortex,* and finally the *cuticle* or scaly outer cover.

Microscopically, the crime investigator will first determine the *Medullary Index* of hairs found at the crime scene. The Index is defined as the width of the medulla divided by the width of the cortex. *Figure 26* has been worked out for a human and a dog hair. For a human being, the Medullary Index is never greater than .3, while no animal hair is ever less than .5.

IDENTIFYING FOODS—A SPOT OF COFFEE

The groceries in the kitchen will now be the subject of microscopic investigation. *Figure 27* will be your guide in

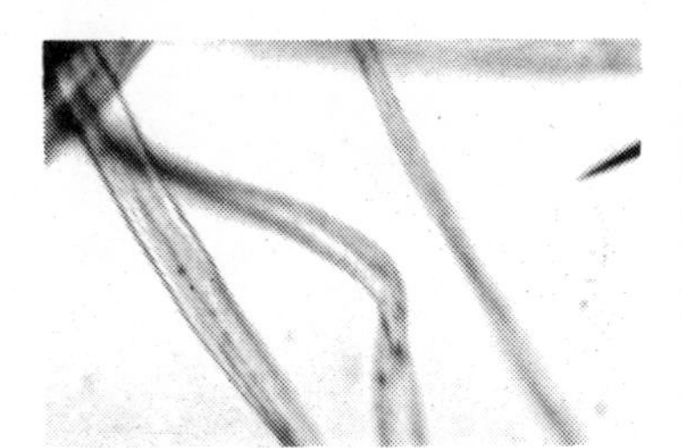

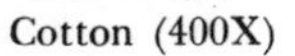

Cotton (400X)

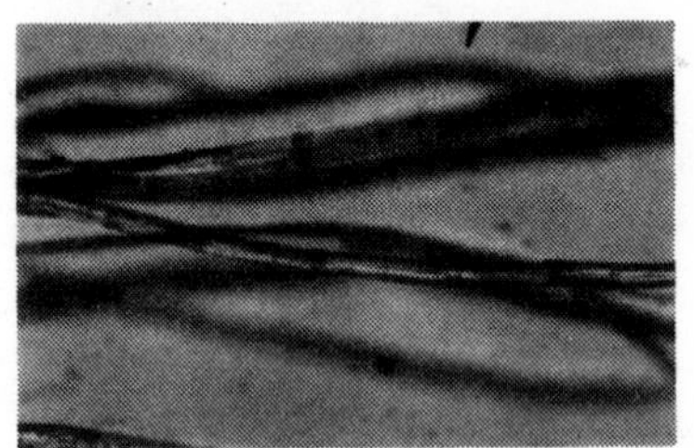

Linen (400X)

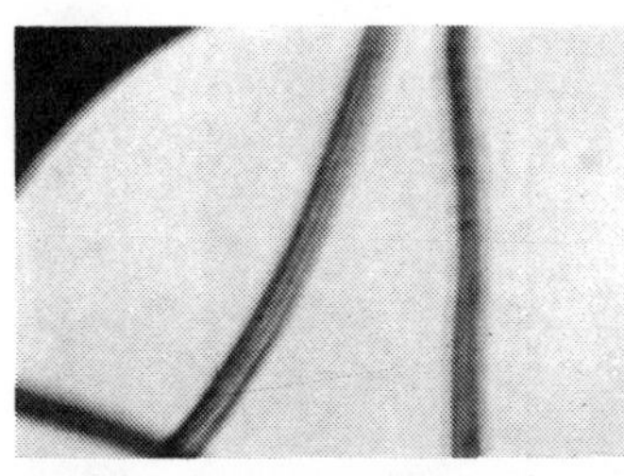

Silk (400X)

Wool (400X)

Polyester (400X)

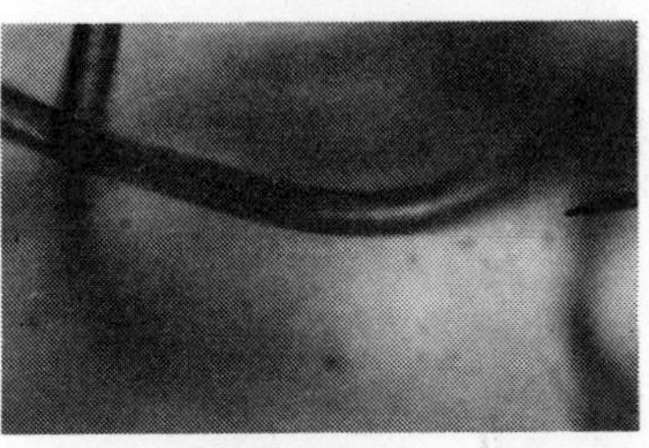

Nylon (400X)

Fig. 25. Identifying fibers under the microscope.

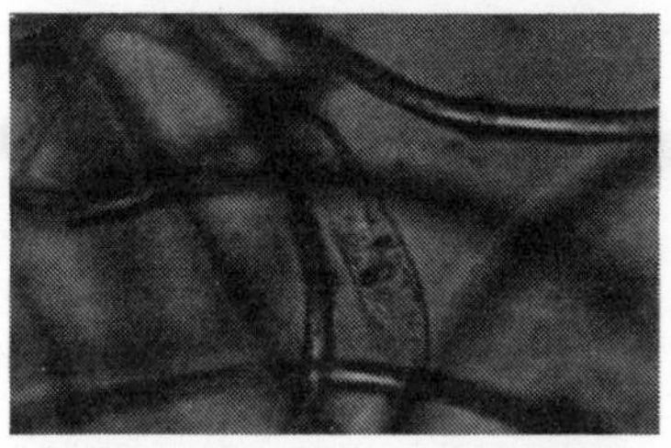

65% Polyester/35% Cotton (400X)

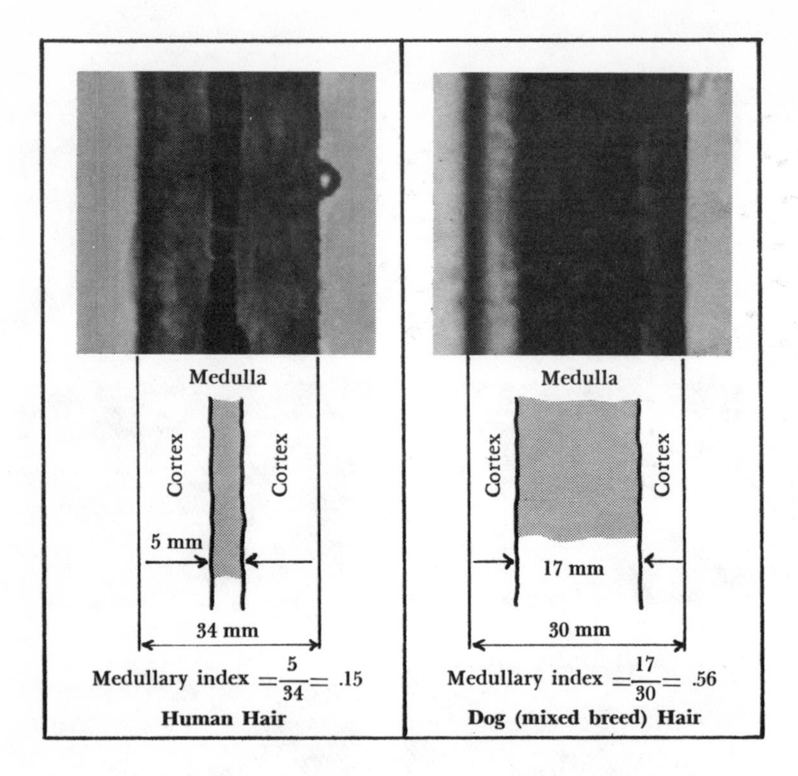

Fig. 26. Comparing the human hair and the dog hair at 400X.

learning the appearance and structure of coffee.

The ground coffee bean is made up of a firm network that encloses cells filled with a granular material containing minute drops of oil (see *Figure 28*). The outline of each cell is wavy because of the irregular swellings in the network surrounding it.

Particles of ground coffee are easy to distinguish from instant coffee under the microscope because instant coffee

Fig. 27.
The structure of coffee.

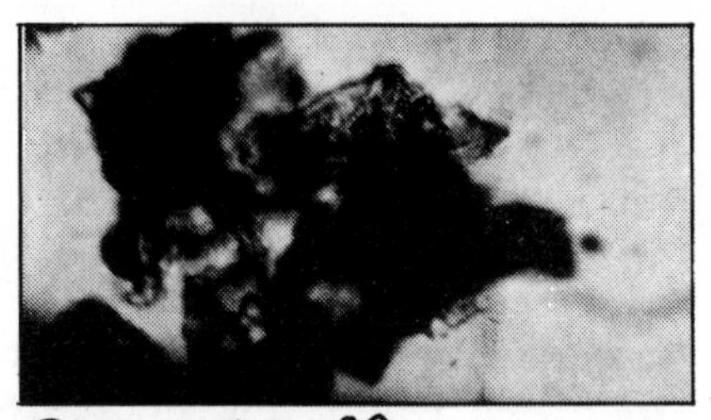

Ground Coffee

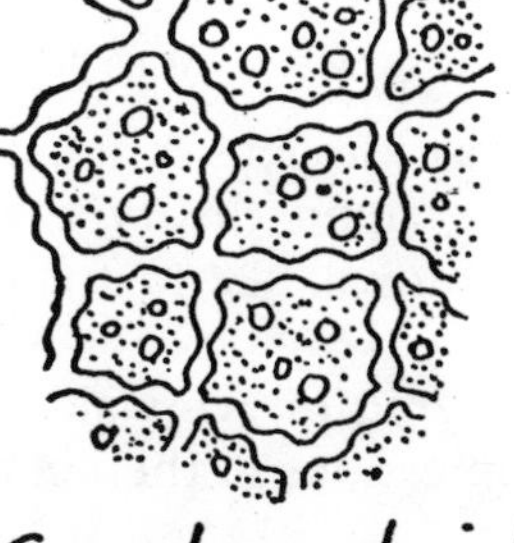

Granular material containing minute drops of oil.

Instant Coffee

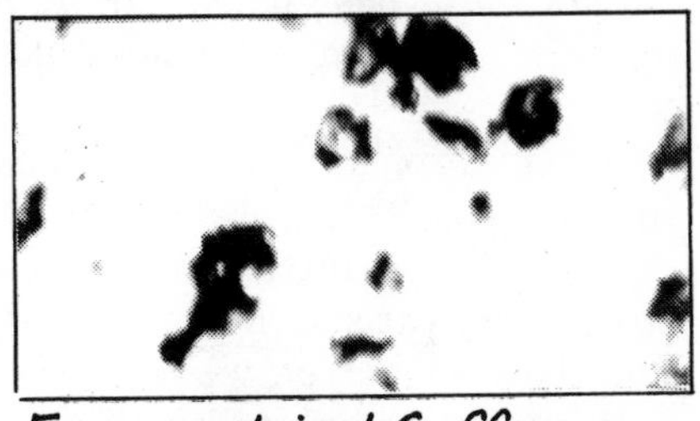

Freeze-dried Coffee

appears as uniform, brownish crystals without any of the cellular structure or oil droplets present in ground coffee.

The appearance of instant coffee is what we would expect when its method of manufacture is considered. Ground coffee is brewed under controlled conditions in a number of steps. During each additional step, more fresh-brewed coffee is added, making it stronger and stronger. Then the extract is dried, either on a hot surface to form a powder, or sprayed into a current of hot air to form beads. In either case, only the liquid extracted from the coffee bean cell is dried, leaving behind the cells or oil droplets seen in ground coffee.

Crystals of freeze-dried coffee look similar to instant coffee crystals. But the particles of freeze-dried coffee are smaller in size and more transparent than instant coffee (see *Figure 27*). During the freeze-drying process, the coffee extract is frozen into slabs. The slabs are then ground into smaller pieces and placed in low pressure chambers where the moisture is removed as a gas. Dry crystals of coffee are left.

STARCH GRAINS—NOW YOU SEE THEM, NOW YOU DON'T

One of the basic foods found in most kitchens is starch, and its appearance differs depending upon the type of starch it is. By looking at *Figure 28* you will see that corn starch differs from potato starch.

Corn starch has grains that are *polyhedral,* or many-sided, in shape and have small cross-like depressions in their centers.

Potato starch has larger granules, and each particle shows irregular concentric oval rings.

For many plants, starch is the way reserve energy is stored. We eat starch foods in order to get that energy for ourselves. However, we must first digest that starch to convert it to sugar before it will do us any good. Starch digestion begins in the mouth and can be seen under the microscope.

Saliva contains an enzyme, *ptyalin* (salivary amylase), that speeds up the change of starch to sugar. This process can actually be observed under the microscope. Transfer a tiny amount of starch to a shallow well slide using a toothpick. Make a note of the size, shape, and approximate number of starch grains. Place a small amount of saliva in the depression of the slide next to the starch grains. Collect

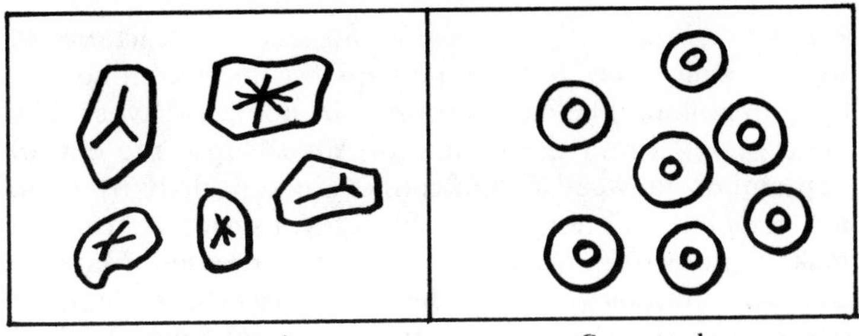

Fig. 28. Structure of starches.

the saliva sample before eating. Chewing on a clean rubber band is a simple way to cause your mouth to fill with saliva. Cover the depression with a cover glass or a plastic coverslip. Keep the slide in a warm place because *ptyalin* works best at body temperature. Examine the slide at five-minute intervals for 45 minutes and look for changes in the size, shape, and number of starch grains.

DETECTING POLLEN FROM VARIOUS PLANTS

Another specialty for which extensive use has been found in actual criminal detective work is the classifying of the hundreds of varieties of pollen from the stamens of plants.

Under the microscope you will find that the forms of the pollen grains are almost as sharply differentiated as the flowers of the plant from which the pollen comes. Some are amazingly sculptured, covered with spinous projections, or otherwise characterized.

A good way to study pollen is to collect it from the various flowers and place it in small labeled envelopes. Make a permanent mount for each kind in Canada Balsam and label it correctly.

Pollen grains are responsible for allergic reactions in some people. Hay fever is perhaps the most common allergy to pollen. The culprit is *ragweed*, not hay (hay is really dried grass). From the middle of August until the end of September, ragweed pollen counts are kept daily by some hospitals for the information of hay fever sufferers. You can make your own count during the hay fever season. Mark off an area, 5 mm. by 5 mm., in the center of a clean slide. Coat that space with a very thin coating of petroleum jelly (Vaseline), then leave the slide on a window ledge or other area where it will be exposed to the air. After three hours, examine the marked part of the slide with the microscope and count the number of pollen grains. Do this daily during the hay fever season and record your results. How do your counts compare to the official counts in your area?

THE ARCHES, LOOPS, AND WHORLS OF FINGERPRINTS

This is a vast subject and many books have been devoted to this specialty. You can, however, learn enough in a few minutes to begin to examine fingerprints with a good pocket lens or the low power of your microscope.

Look at your fingertips. The raised lines are called *ridges* and the depressions between them are called *furrows*. Both form a pattern that is uniquely yours. Your fingerprints are different than anybody else's in the whole world! The standard groups of fingerprints used by the FBI are pictured in *Figure 29*.

All you need to make a set of fingerprints is some white paper and a stamp pad. Press your index finger (the one next to your thumb) firmly onto the stamp pad. Be sure you ink part of the middle joint as well as the tip. Carefully lay the *left* side of your index finger down first, then roll your finger slowly over until it is resting on its right side. Lift it up and away from the paper. The impression should be clear, complete, and unsmudged. What you just did was *roll* a fingerprint exactly as the police or the FBI do. Try

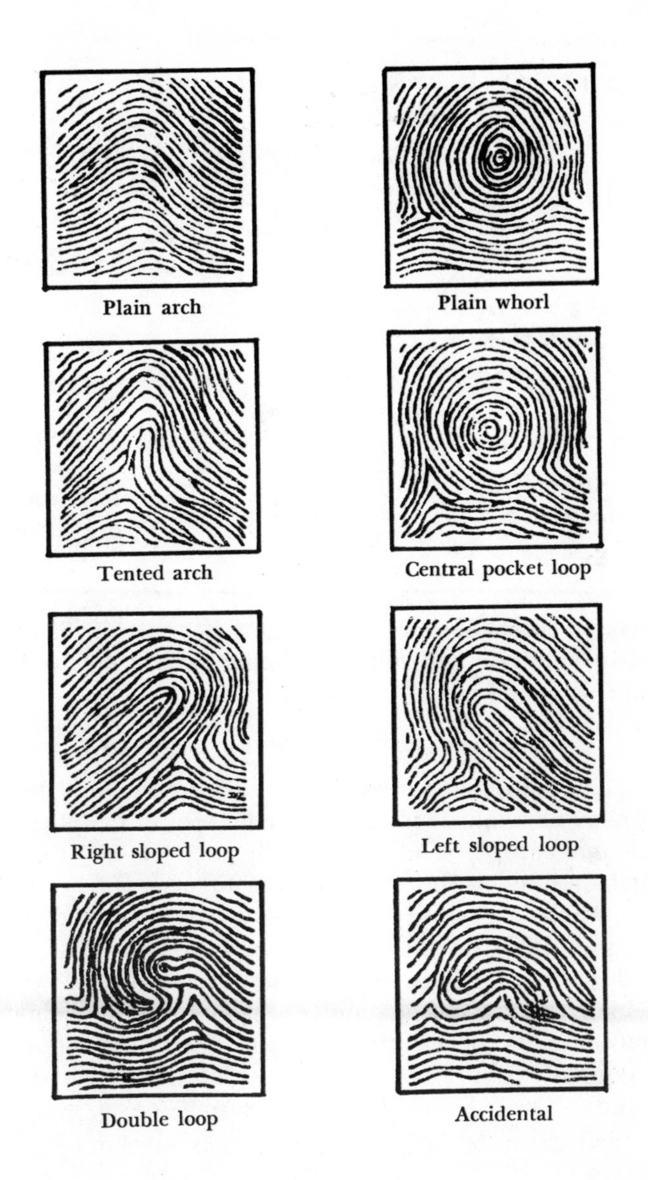

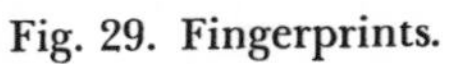
Fig. 29. Fingerprints.

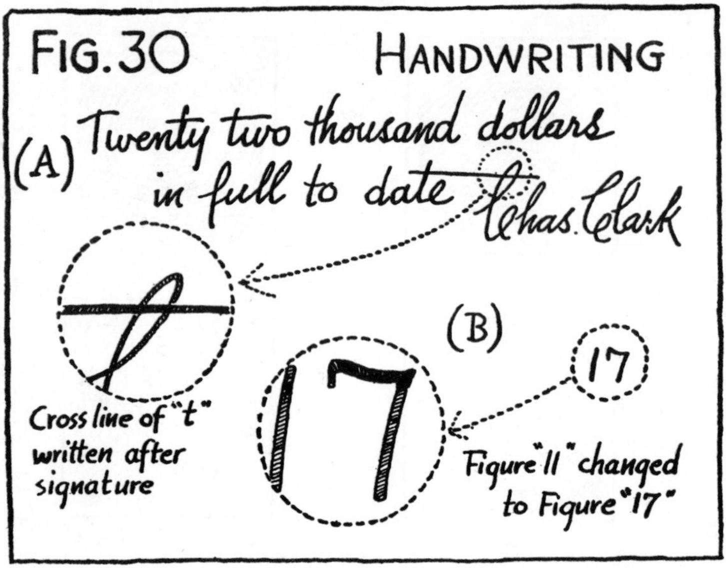

FIG. 30 HANDWRITING

(A) Twenty two thousand dollars in full to date Chas. Clark

Cross line of "t" written after signature

(B) Figure "11" changed to Figure "17"

making prints of your other fingers (for the left hand, start with right side and roll left), being careful not to use too much ink and not to smudge the prints.

DETECTING HANDWRITING FORGERIES

Handwriting experts are often called upon for expert testimony at criminal trials. The main tool of every expert is his microscope. Under a magnification of only 50 or 100 diameters even the most perfect forgery of a signature or alteration in a figure on a check reveals characteristics that frequently expose its false nature to the viewer.

Figure 30 gives two illustrations of the ways in which the microscope proves useful in establishing the genuineness or falsity of "questioned documents." In example A, it was required to determine whether the words "in full to date," appearing on a note were **added after or before the note was signed by Charles Clark.**

With the naked eye it was impossible to tell, but the microscope showed that the crossing of the "t" in "date" was written across the "C" in "Charles," proving that a crime had been committed by the alteration of the note after it was signed by its maker.

The other example, (B), shows how the microscope revealed that the 7 of 17 was made by altering the second 1 of 11.

To the naked eye the faked 7 was undetectable, and looked as if made without raising the pen from the paper, as a person naturally writes a "7."

But the microscope showed that the pen had been lifted after adding the top of the "7" to a "1" which was already on the paper.

The use of the microscope in detective work has recently made great strides, and has furnished evidence resulting in the punishment of crimes which would have gone scot-free for lack of proof only a few years ago.

DETECTING PAPER MATERIALS

The first paper in the world was the papyrus of the Egyptians—and if it had remained the only paper, we should have no need for studying the various materials with a view to detecting them in unknown samples.

Papyrus was built up from the thin skin of the stems of the papyrus plant. This tissue was peeled off, and the resulting strips were laid crosswise to form woven sheets. After drying under pressure, the papyrus paper was ready to write on with a brush or reed pen. Papyrus was widely used, because it was much cheaper than parchment, the dried skin of animals.

Paper, as we know it today, was invented by the Chinese. The first material was cotton, but they also used the pulp of mulberry or other woods, straw, and vegetable stems. Linen came into use as paper material in the middle ages and was used in Arabia in 1100 A.D.

The use of wood-pulp from forest trees as material for cheap paper was suggested by the French naturalist Reamur. He had watched wasps building a paper nest from the wood-fibres they scraped from fence posts and other exposed wood, "Why not do likewise?", thought Reamur, and as a result we have modern newspapers and a whole class of cheap magazines called "the pulps."

In the process of making wood pulp paper the finely shredded wood is heated with strong alkali, reduced to a creamy paste and then washed free of the alkali. This semi-liquid wood is then spread out on rollers to a thin sheet, and gradually dried.

Many other materials are also used for various kinds of paper, including corn-husks, straw, sawdust, etc. Accordingly, it often becomes of commercial importance to be able to detect the materials composing any given sample. For this work the microscope is the most important aid.

To prepare paper for microscopic examination first tear it into very small bits, and boil them for a few minutes in a weak (1 per cent) solution of caustic soda. Then wash thoroughly on a fine sieve, and shake the resulting pulp in a test-tube of clean water. From this you can transfer a drop or two of the milky liquid to a slide for examination.

Identification of the materials composing the sample of paper is made by noting the size and shape of the wood-cells, their length, width compared to length, shape of the ends, etc. A few characteristics of the commonest paper materials—wood and straw—now follow.

The trees used for paper materials are of two main

sorts. One kind embraces the pine family, including spruce, fir, pine, balsam, larch and hemlock. Scientists call them the conifers (cone-bearers) or *gymnosperms*. The other kind includes the poplar and birch, which are called *angiosperms*.

The wood-pulp paper you have prepared into a milky fluid for examination under your microscope is filled with cells called *tracheids*. Their appearance under the microscope is indicated by the drawings (*A*) and (*B*) in *Figure 31*. The two kinds furnished by gymnosperm and angiosperm trees are very characteristic, so that you will have little difficulty in identifying them.

(A) *Gymnosperm cells* (Pine, Fir, Spruce, etc.) are long, often extending clear across and out of the low-power field of your microscope. The ends are fairly sharp. The characteristics identifying features are round or oval markings in regular rows which run *lengthwise* of the cells. The sketch indicates both oval and round marks, which often both occur in a single cell.

(B) *Angiosperm cells* (Poplar and Birch) are smaller and broader, and pointed at both ends. Their characteristic markings are rows of tiny dots, or minute pores, which are arranged in rows running *crosswise* of the cells. These angiosperm cells are seen in the microscope field mixed up with long narrow fibres without any characteristic markings.

(C) *Straw cells*. The pulp from paper made from straw and other grass stems contains long slender fibres knotted at regular intervals. These are frequently pointed at the ends, and have a narrow canal inside, which is constricted at each knot. For straw pulp you will also see cells from the outer skin of the stems and cells from the inner or pith layer of the straw. (See *Figure 31*.)

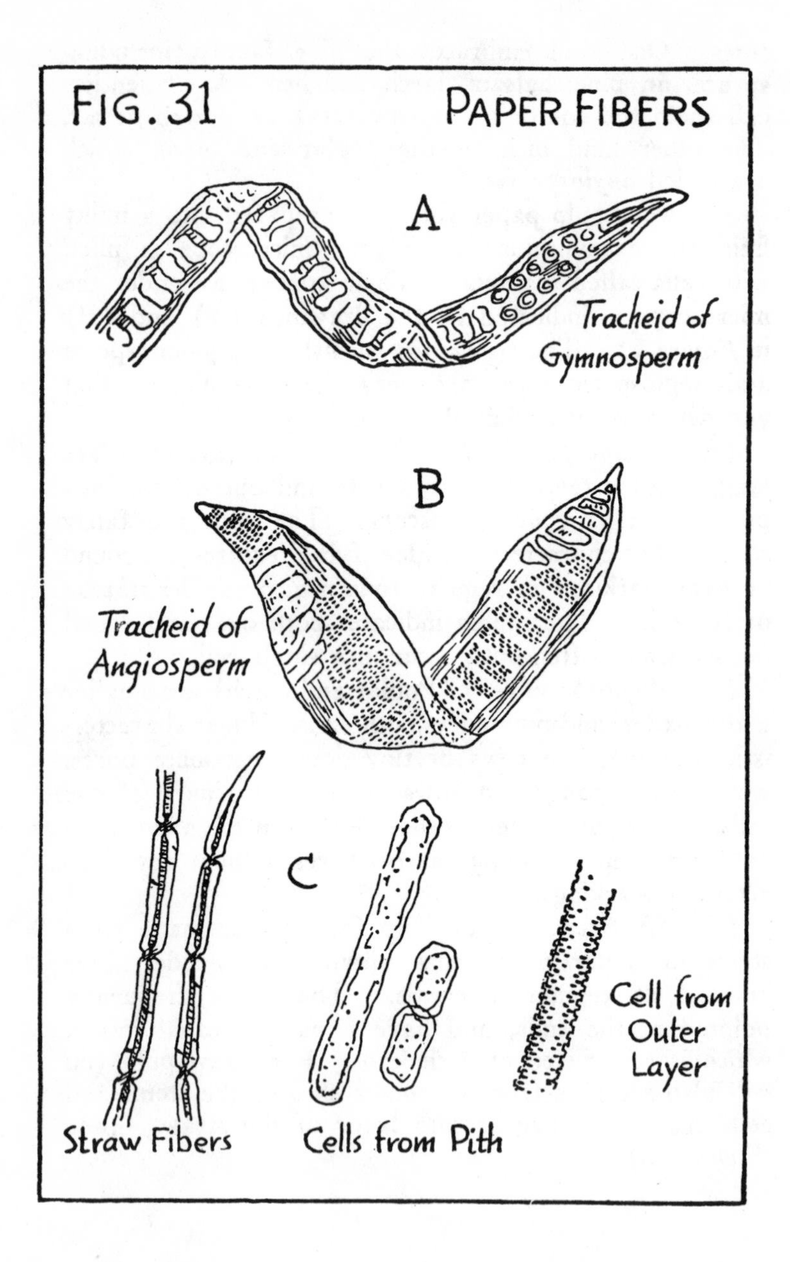
FIG. 31
PAPER FIBERS
A
Tracheid of
Gymnosperm
B
Tracheid of
Angiosperm
C
Straw Fibers
Cells from Pith
Cell from
Outer
Layer

MICROSCOPIC EXAMINATION OF URINE

This branch of medical science is extremely important in life insurance and in diagnosing many diseased conditions of the kidneys and other organs. We can give only a hint of some of the most characteristic things which you may see when examining a sample of urine under your microscope.

First allow it to settle in a test-tube until the solid matter is accumulated at the bottom. Then draw off a few drops of this with a pointed glass dipping tube or medicine dropper.

The principal objects which you may see are crystals, red and white blood cells, epithelial cells (from the lining of the kidney) and "tube-casts." These features are identified for your eye at (*A*) in *Figure 32*.

The crystals are *uric acid, acid urates, calcium oxalate* and *ammonium magnesium phosphate. Uric acid* occurs in clusters of rhombic (diamond shape) prisms, which sometimes look like tiny whetstones.

Acid urates are seen in formless, granular masses.

Calcium oxalate occurs in octahedral (eight-sided) crystals. In some positions they show four shapes like the areas on the back of a straight-flap envelope.

Ammonium magnesium phosphate is identified by its long or short prisms with beveled edges, appearing something like square-cut jewels. They are also called "coffin-shaped."

The blood cells are either "white" or "red." The white are much larger. *Epithelial* cells are still larger, and show a prominent central spot or "nucleus." They are shed from the lining of the kidney. *Tube casts* are clear, glass-like rods which are formed in the kidney tubes by some diseased conditions, and then expelled into the urine.

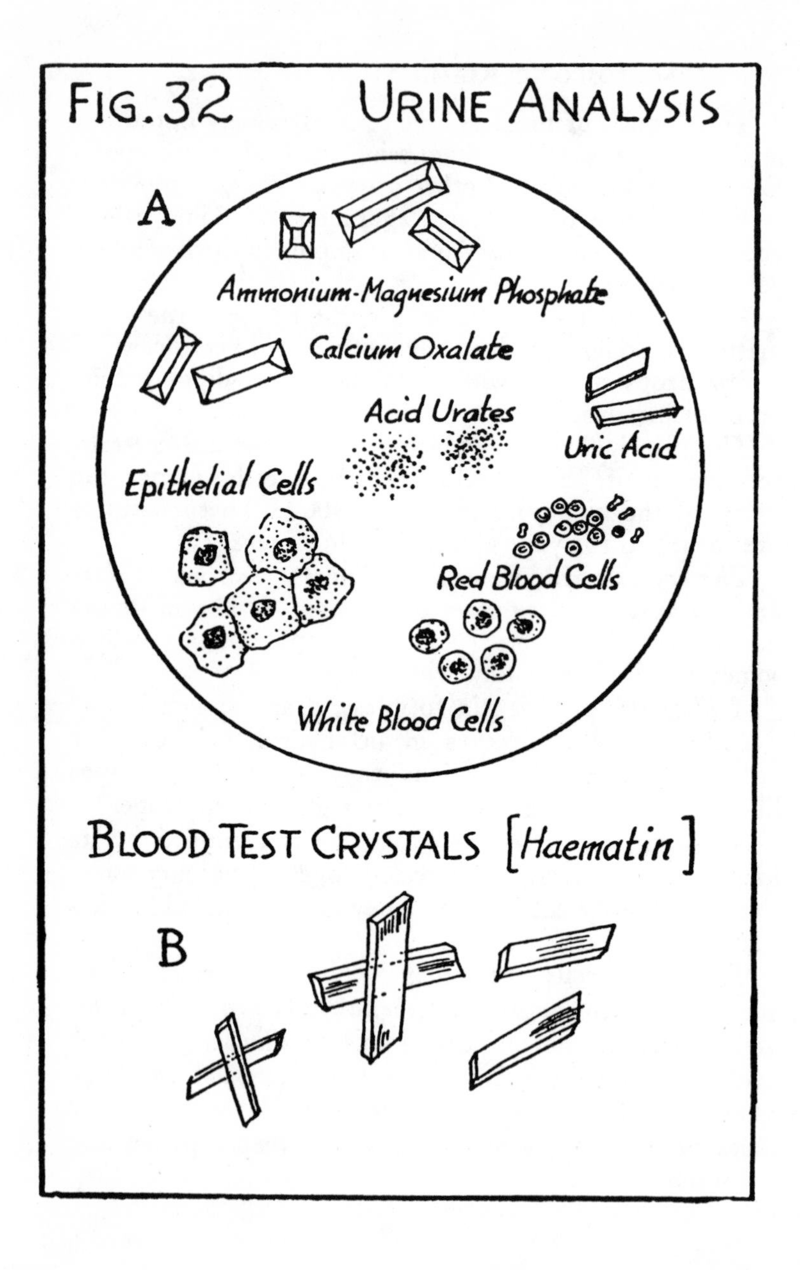
FIG. 32 URINE ANALYSIS
A
Ammonium-Magnesium Phosphate
Calcium Oxalate
Acid Urates
Uric Acid
Epithelial Cells
Red Blood Cells
White Blood Cells
BLOOD TEST CRYSTALS [Haematin]
B

A SIMPLE MICRO-CHEMICAL TEST FOR IDENTIFYING BLOODSTAINS

Here we are entering the field of the scientific detective who is required to give evidence that a murder has been committed! To decide whether or not a given stain is blood is not difficult. To identify blood by a simple micro-chemical test proceed as follows:

Scrape off on a slide a little of the dried stain which is suspected of being blood. If the stain is on wood, you will have to scrape off a few wood fibres along with the dried blood. If on cloth, you may have to cut a little of the cloth. This, however, will not interfere with the test.

To the dried blood on the slide add a drop or two of "glacial acetic acid." This is obtainable from druggists or photo-supply houses. Holding it high over a gas stove, warm the slide with the blood and acid until the acid is entirely evaporated.

The next step is to place a few drops of a very weak solution of common salt on the slide and heat carefully until entirely evaporated. Do not allow the temperature of the slide to exceed 120 degrees Fahrenheit. The correct strength of the salt solution is seven-hundredths of one per cent (0.07%).

To prepare the salt solution: Dissolve in one ounce of water all the salt it will take up. Allow undissolved salt to settle, and draw off a little of this saturated salt solution with a medicine dropper. Place in a test tube. Then add six drops of salt solution to a pint of water (16 ounces). This will be near enough for practical purposes. Place some of this diluted salt solution in a bottle and keep it to make blood tests with.

After the salt solution is entirely evaporated from the slide, place upon it another drop of the glacial acetic acid. This time you must cautiously heat the slide until the drop of acid boils. It will then evaporate very

quickly. When dry and cool, examine the slide under the highest power of your microscope, and look for the characteristic crystals of "*haemin*" which indicate the presence of blood. (See (*B*) in *Figure 32.*)

Haemin crystals are minute flat rhomboids (diamond shaped) often lying in the form of a short-armed cross.

This test is very sensitive and delicate. It will show the presence of as little as one-twentieth of a milligram of dried blood! The age of the stain does not matter either. In a famous murder case the stains upon some legal papers were proved by this test to be blood—although over sixty years had elapsed!

This is not, however, a test for *human* blood; it merely proves that a certain stain was made by the blood of an animal. The test for human blood is not microscopic in character, unless the individual cells can be obtained fresh. If the stain has dried, a difficult serum test is required, which is beyond the reach of an amateur. You can, however, become expert in detecting the presence of blood, and this alone might sometime give important legal evidence.

These few pages give only a few hints of the possibilities which anyone can develop with a microscope and some leisure time to devote to microscopic detective work.

VII
LOOKING AT CELLS

Over three hundred years ago, Robert Hooke, an English scientist who wrote the first book on microscopic observations, *Micrographia*, was looking at a thin slice of cork with a microscope. What he saw resembled the rooms or *cells* of a monastery. He therefore gave the name *cells* to the little spaces that were arranged in order in the cork. Since that time, it has been found that all living things are made of cells. Today, it is known that cells contain living substance and are not the empty spaces that Hooke saw in the cork.

Cut a very thin section of a piece of cork with a sharp razor blade. Place it on a slide and examine the thinnest part with a microscope. You too will be able to see the tiny, even, empty spaces that Hooke aptly named cells.

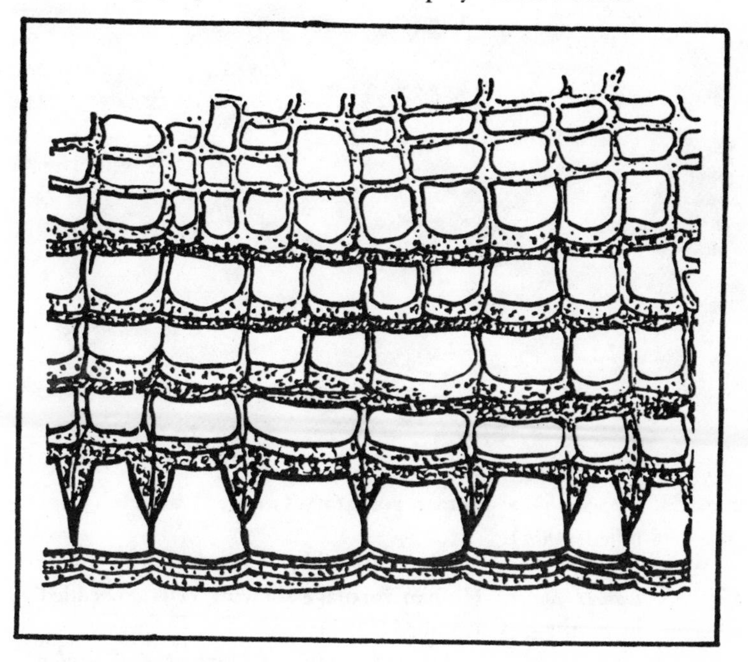

Fig. 33. **This is how a section of cork looks under the microscope.**

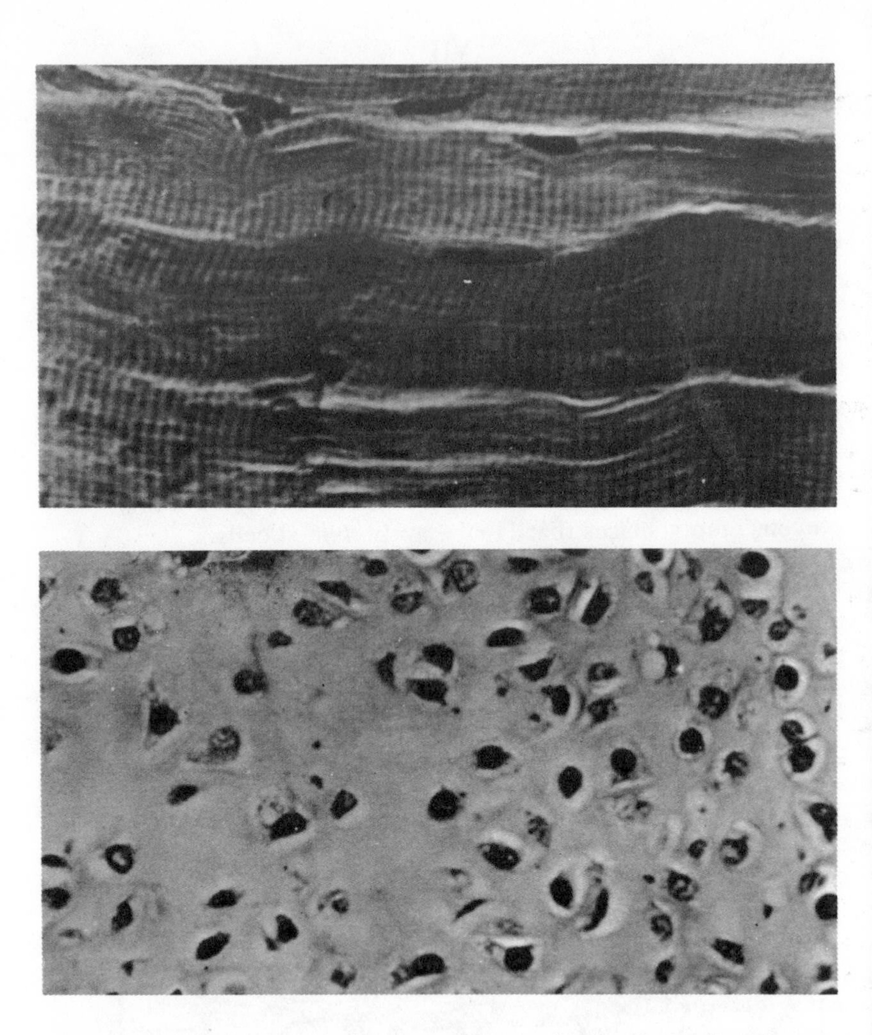

Fig. 34. *Upper photo:* Human voluntary (striated) muscle (magnified 400x).

Courtesy of Herbert A. Fischler

Fig. 35. *Lower photo:* Human cartilage showing cells embedded in cartilage (magnified 385x).

Courtesy of Herbert A. Fischler

RED ONION CELLS

For a view of the living material within cells examine the Bermuda or red onion. You can get one at any vegetable store. Remove a few of the dry outer leaves (scales) and cut out a small section containing the inner purplish membrane. Using a tweezer, peel off a small section of the membrane. Place it on a clean slide, add two or three drops of water, and cover with a cover glass. Under low power, you will see some of the cells filled with a purplish pigment as well as unpigmented cells. Notice their shape. In some of the cells you will see a small circular area filled with tiny granules (see *Figure 36A*). This is the nucleus. Under high power, the nucleus will be clearly seen.

There is a way of making the parts of cells more distinct. If a dye or stain is added to the cells, the parts become more visible. A common and useful stain is Lugol's iodine. When this is added to the slide, the nucleus becomes sharply defined. You can actually see the structure of the nucleus, including one or more nucleoli inside, under the high power. The cytoplasm, the part of the cell on the outside of the nucleus, also becomes more clearly defined. It is present as very fine granules distributed throughout the inside of the cell.

Both the nucleus and the cytoplasm are living parts of the cell. These two parts together with the cell membrane that covers the outside of the cytoplasm make up the living substance of the cell. On the outside is the non-living cell wall. This supports the cell and gives it its shape.

You may not be able to see the cell membrane because it is pushed right up against the cell wall. There is, however, a way of separating it from the cell wall so that it can be easily seen. Make up a salt solution by adding a teaspoon of salt to half a glass of water. Add two drops of this solution to a piece of fresh red onion membrane placed on a clean slide. Cover with a cover glass. After several minutes you will notice that the cell contents are shrinking away from

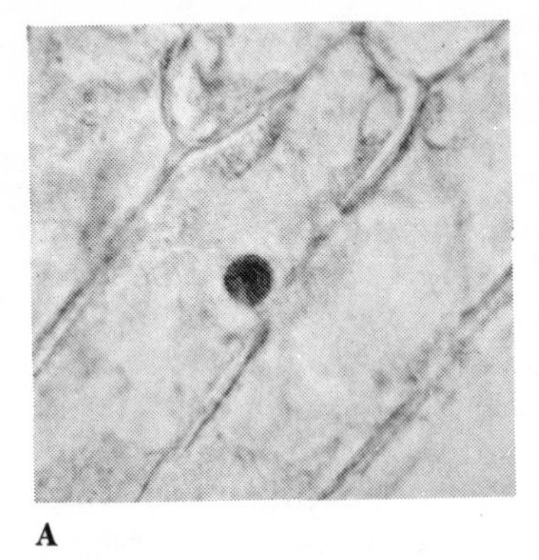

A

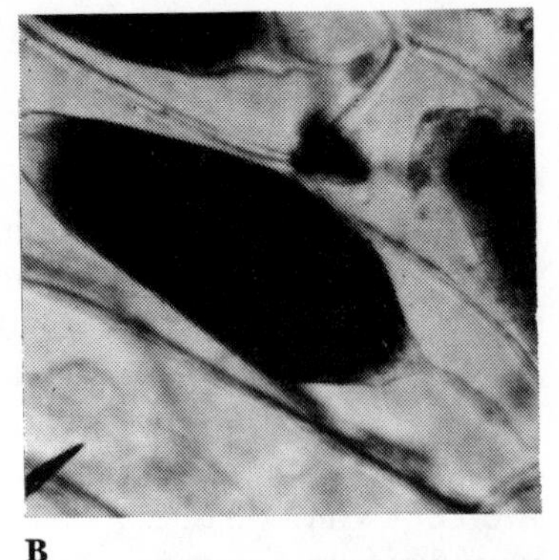

B

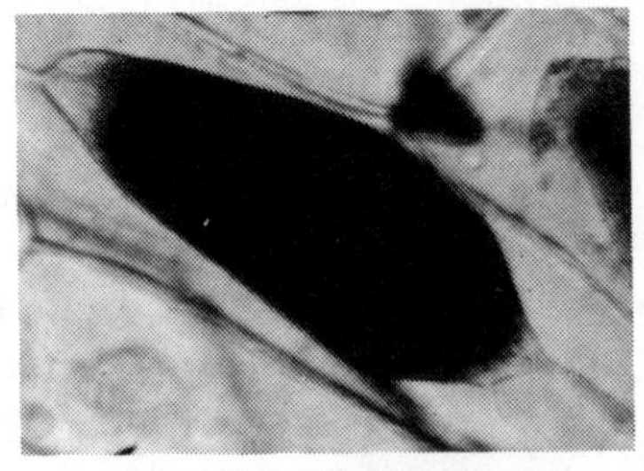

A. Red onion skin in Lugol's iodine solution (400X).

B. Red onion skin cells in salt solution (400X).

C. Structure of the red onion skin cell.

Fig. 36. Red onion skin.

the cell wall (see *Figure 36 B*). Now you will be able to see the cell membrane on the outside of the cytoplasm. In *Figure 36 B*, you can see the cell contents in the center of the cell and the cell membrane is clearly visible. If you look carefully, you can see the nucleus because it is lighter in appearance than the surrounding pigment. The nucleus is in a straight line with the pointer. Notice how the cell membrane remains attached to the cell wall on both short ends of the cell.

CHEEK CELLS

You can easily see some of the cells that make up the cheek lining by making a slide in the following way. Gently scrape the inside of your cheek two or three times with the broad end of a toothpick. Then spread the wet material across a clean slide, without applying too much pressure. Since these cells are being transferred away from their natural position, their shape will become distorted if you apply too much pressure when placing them on the slide. Now, add a drop or two of methylene blue or Lugol's iodine stain; ordinary ink that has been filtered may also be used. Carefully place a cover slip over it, and examine with the low power.

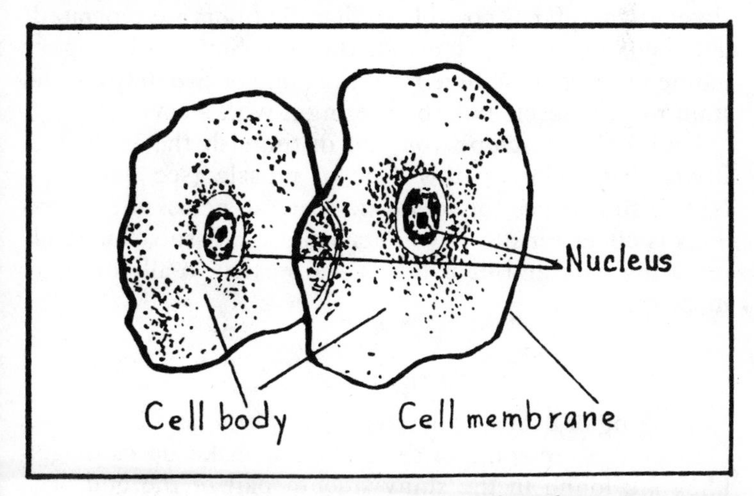

Fig. 37. Cheek cells seen under the microscope.

Under the microscope, you will see small collections of cells. Look for little masses that have been stained by the dye. These cells are quite small. Notice their five-sided shape. Compare several cells in order to make out the general shape. See how the cells are attached to each other. Do you see the nucleus in the center of each? It has a deeper color.

Under the high power, you can see more of the details. The outside of the cell is the cell membrane. The granular material within it is the cytoplasm. You will probably see the granules that make up the nucleus, too.

MUSCLE CELLS

Another type of cell is found in the muscles of your arms or legs. These muscles that you can move at will are called *voluntary muscles*. Similar muscle tissue can be seen in a small sliver of beef. To make a slide take a piece of frozen beef and scrape a thin sliver, using a razor blade. Spread the sliver apart as far as possible so that the fibers are separated. Two pins make ideal tools for this job. Stain with Lugol's iodine or methylene blue by adding one or two drops of the stain to the muscle before covering it with a cover glass.

Under the miscrope you can distinguish the individual fibers that make up this type of muscle (see page 94). Notice the stripes, or *striations*, that run across the fibers. This is characteristic of voluntary muscle tissue. These alternating dark and light bands are present in all voluntary muscles.

CARTILAGE

Speaking of beef, if you have a part of the end of a bone, you can also see some of the cells that make up cartilage. They are found in the shiny smooth part of the end of a bone. With a sharp razor, slice away a small portion of this cartilage—the thinner the better. Add a stain to it on a slide, cover, and then examine with the microscope. You can see the cells scattered amidst the solid material that makes up the cartilage. Each cell is in a little space, and they are generally found in pairs. They seem almost like islands in a sea of hard material.

VIII

MICROSCOPIC PETS

THE PARAMECIUM

How would you like to raise a microscopic pet? It may be too small to play with or handle, but it can be watched and studied on the stage of a microscope as it moves rapidly hither and yon. The paramecium is one of the most common of all one-celled animals. You will have little difficulty finding it in any pond water (see *Figure 38*).

To grow paramecium culture at home, this is all you have to do. Obtain a brewer's yeast tablet at a drug store, and crumble it in a glass of water. Then, add some water taken from a pond, containing paramecium, to this glass; a half full medicine-dropper will be enough. Put the glass aside in a shaded spot. In about a week, if you hold the glass up to the light, you will see it swarming with tiny specks that are moving about. These are the paramecia.

Place a drop of the culture on a slide. You will see a mob scene of paramecia, twisting, turning, and darting about. They move so quickly that you will have to keep moving the slide in order to be able to follow them.

You will undoubtedly want to slow them down. One of the best ways of doing this is to take a small piece of lens paper, about a centimeter square, and pull it apart very carefully. Just before the two ends come apart, place it on a slide, and then add your drop of culture at the spot where the two parts have almost separated. Under the microscope, you will see that the paramecia have become trapped. They keep bumping into the fibers of the lens paper. This compels them to stay in a smaller area of the slide, and enables you to get a better look at them.

Now you can see how it appears to glide along. It is propelled by little hair-like projections called cilia, which surround it on all sides. These cilia beat like so many oars, and propel the paramecium in quick darts. It may be easier to see the beating cilia if you reduce the amount of light striking the slide, by adjusting the diaphragm. A higher magnification, of course, also helps.

How does the paramecium eat? You will see how food particles enter, if you add some carmine particles to a small amount of the culture. These particles do not dissolve in the water, but remain suspended as tiny grains. Under the high power, look at the middle part of a paramecium that has stopped moving for a while. You will see a funnel-like section that has beating cilia. This is the mouth. The movement of the cilia creates a current that sweeps in any small materials nearby. As these particles are swept in, you will see them collect at the end of the mouth tube into a small food vacuole. This grows to a certain size, and becomes detached. It then moves around within the protoplasm of the paramecium. You will probably see many of these food vacuoles inside one paramecium. The food is digested there.

You will be interested in seeing the "stinging hairs" or *trichocysts* of a paramecium. Place a drop of ordinary fountain-pen ink on a slide, together with a drop of paramecium culture. Add a cover slip. You will notice that the paramecia have been killed by the ink. However, before they died, they shot out many of these long hairs which you now see on the micro-organism. It is thought by scientists that the paramecium uses these long hairs to protect itself against other tiny animals that may be annoying it. The irritating material or trichocysts keeps them away.

Courtesy of American Museum of Natural History

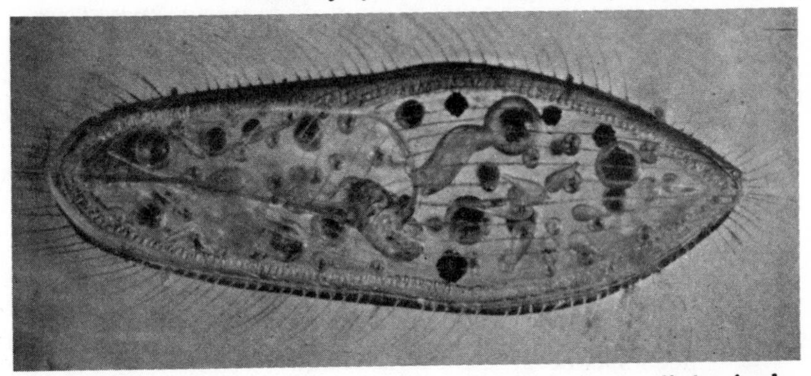

Fig. 38. The Paramecium, one of the most common of one-celled animals.

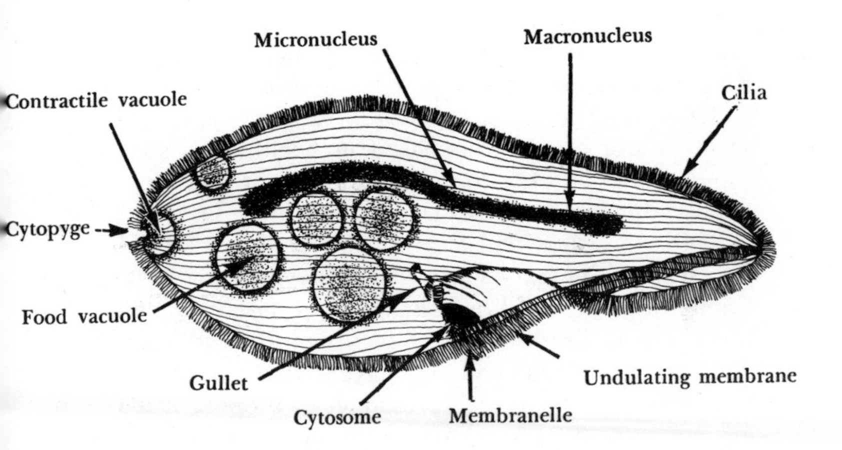

Fig. 39. The Blepharisma, a relative of the Parmecium that often becomes a cannibal.

When a paramecium has grown to its full size it begins to reproduce. It does this by splitting into two separate parts. Each part then swims away as a completely new paramecium. When conditions are right, a paramecium reproduces in this way every hour. At this rate, you can imagine how many can be formed in a day. The number runs into the millions. You will often be able to see a paramecium in the process of reproducing when you examine a thick culture.

THE BLEPHARISMA

Paramecium are nice but *Blepharisma* make better specimens because they swim slower and have a pink color that makes them easier to see. They are also much larger than the paramecium. Blephs, as they are often called, are usually found on the bottom of fresh-water ponds. Like their relative the paramecium, they use their cilia for feeding and moving about.

It is not difficult to provide a home and food for the Blepharisma. Dissolve a powdered cereal green tablet in half a glass of boiled spring water. Cereal green tablets and spring water can be purchased in health food stores and some supermarkets. Pour the mixture into test tubes and expose the test tubes to the air for three days. Now add your Blephs; they will feed on the bacteria that will have grown in the cereal "soup." Keep your Blephs away from bright sunlight. In dim light they can last for many days, but if left in bright sunlight they will die within an hour.

After a few weeks you may have to transfer the Blephs to a new home. Continue to feed your Blephs; if a Blepharisma culture is starved, some members will become cannibals and feed on their relatives. It is easy to spot the cannibals since they are usually twice as big as those that feed on bacteria.

IX

BLOOD — THE LIFE STREAM

The chance are that the only time you have ever seen blood is when you cut your finger, and some of the blood flowed out. How would you like to watch blood flowing around within the blood vessels? Your microscope can reveal this sight to you, just as it first did for Leeuwenhoek, over three hundred years ago.

All you really need is a medium-sized goldfish. First prepare a piece of absorbent cotton about two inches square. Soak it under the faucet so that it is full of water. Remove the goldfish from the water and wrap its head and the front part of its body in the soaked absorbent cotton. If the cotton surrounds these parts of the fish thoroughly, it can be kept alive out of water for as much as twenty minutes.

Now, place the fish on a small glass plate large enough to cover the stage of the microscope. If you have a petri dish, you can use half of it to hold the fish. Now spread out the tail of the fish on the glass. Examine it with the low power of the microscope. If the fish flips its tail out of focus, it would be a good idea to hold the tail in place with half of a microscope slide.

Look for the blood circulating within the small blood vessels. The tiny round structures are the blood cells. Notice how many of them there are. There are millions! In some of the blood vessels, they pass along in single file. These are the smallest blood vessels, the capillaries. As you trace a capillary along, you will see that it connects with another capillary, or else it may join a larger blood vessel, such as a vein or an artery.

Some of the small arteries can be recognized because the blood goes through them in spurts. This is due to the pumping action of the heart. Every time the heart beats, it sends the blood into the arteries which expand under the great pressure, and then relax again to their normal width. This sudden expansion of the artery, each time the heart beats, produces the pulse. The other larger blood vessels through which the blood flows with a steady movement are the veins. As you move the slide around, you can distinguish the three types of blood vessels from each other.

Turn to high power. Now you can see the blood cells a little more clearly. They appear orange-pink in color, and are football-shaped. In the center of each, you can make out the nucleus. These are the red blood cells. When millions of them are gathered into a drop, they make the blood appear red in color. Here and there, you may be able to see other cells being carried along. They are gray in color and may not have any particular shape. These are the white blood cells.

By this time, it may be necessary to return the fish to water. Simply remove the absorbent cotton before you do so. Usually the fish will swim about actively. However, if it floats on its side, you may have to revive it. This can be done by holding the fish's tail, and "dunking" its head in and out of the water about a dozen times. This action causes a fresh supply of water to stream past the gills in a very short time, and helps the fish recover more rapidly.

YOUR OWN BLOOD

If you would like to examine a sample of your own blood, follow this procedure. Swab the tip of your little finger with a piece of absorbent cotton that has been dipped in alcohol. This sterilizes the end of the finger. Pass a needle through a flame once or twice to sterilize it too. After a moment for cooling, prick the soft part of the tip of the finger with the needle. Touch the drop of blood that oozes out to a clean slide. Spread the blood out in a thin film with the edge of the narrow side of another

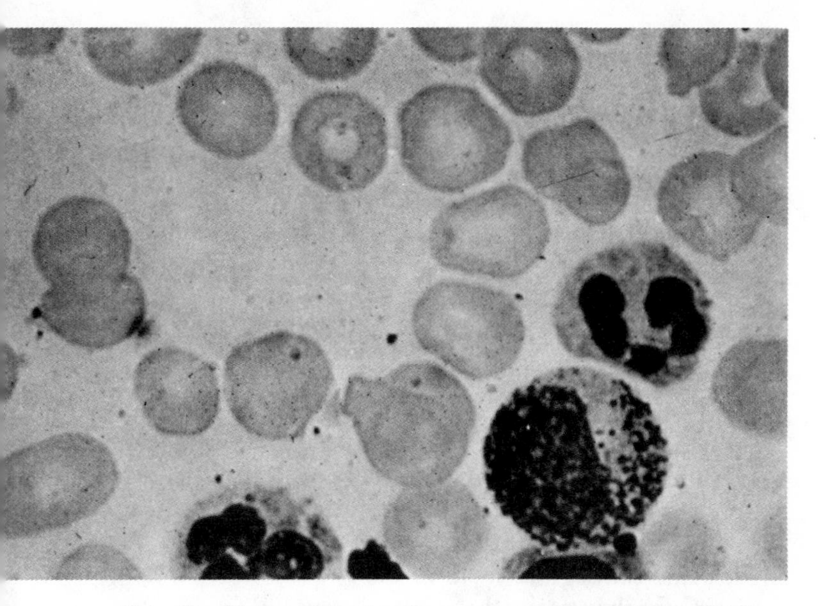

Fig. 40. Human blood cells as seen under oil immersion (magnified 1000x).

Courtesy of Herbert A. Fischler

slide. Allow this smear to dry. Under the high power of the microscope, you will see that the red blood cells are round and pinkish-orange in color. They are shaped like coins (see *Figure 40*). The center part is thinner than the outer edge. There is one unusual feature about human red blood cells; they do not have a nucleus. The blood owes its color to the presence of all these red blood cells. If they were removed from the liquid part of the blood, the plasma, the blood would be straw-colored.

The white blood cells are not as numerous as the red blood cells. They are somewhat larger in size and grayish in color. In most cases they contain a large nucleus. There are several types of white blood cells which an expert can learn to recognize. For anyone interested in studying more about blood cells, there is a special stain called Wright's Stain prepared for this purpose.

X

STARTING THE STUDY OF BACTERIA

You do not need very elaborate equipment to enter the field of bacteriology. A microscope with a high power objective that gives magnifications up to 430 times will be good for many interesting hours spent viewing these tiny organisms.

BACTERIA FROM THE MOUTH

A good place to start is your teeth. Scrape off some of the white material from the molars with a toothpick. Put a drop of water on a slide. Then, spread this material as thinly as you can in this drop of water. When it is dry, "fix" the bacteria by passing the slide quickly through a flame two or three times. This kills the bacteria, and at the same time, glues them to the slide so that they will not wash off when stained.

The slide is then ready to be stained. This is necessary if you are to see the bacteria clearly. Otherwise, they would be colorless, and difficult to observe. The stain dyes them and makes them stand out against a clear background.

A good stain is methylene blue. This can be obtained in a drugstore. Place a drop or two on the part of the slide containing the material from the teeth. Let it remain there for three minutes. Then wash the excess stain off by holding the slide under a gentle flow of water from the faucet.

The slide should be blotted dry between two sheets of filter paper, or allowed to dry in the air. It should *not* be wiped, because wiping will remove the bacteria. A cover slip is not necessary. The slide is now ready to be examined.

Under the high power, you will be able to see the three types of bacteria: the rod-shaped *bacilli;* the round-shaped *cocci;* and the spiral-shaped *spirilla* (see *Fig.* 43–44). These particular bacteria, taken from the teeth, are harmless.

BACTERIA FROM BUTTERMILK

Another good place to find bacteria is in buttermilk. Most of the buttermilk now sold by the large dairies is made by inoculating milk with a type of bacteria called *Streptococcus lactis*. You can buy this buttermilk under the label "cultured." To make a slide of the bacteria, place a drop on a clean slide, and spread it out. After it has dried, place the slide in a small container of alcohol. This removes the fat particles that would otherwise obscure your view of the bacteria. It also fixes the bacteria. After five to ten minutes, stain the slide with methylene blue in the same manner as was done for the teeth bacteria.

When you examine the slide, you will see the chains of round bacteria that are called streptococci. They look like strings of beads. These bacteria are also harmless. As a matter of fact, they are useful to man in that they work for him in the dairy industry to produce buttermilk.

BACTERIA ON PLANT ROOTS

Other useful bacteria are also found growing on the roots of certain plants called legumes, such as beans, clover, and alfalfa. If you carefully dig up one of these plants, so as not to injure the roots, you can wash the soil away gently, and find the little swellings, or nodules on the roots. These nodules contain useful "nitrogen-fixing" bacteria that help provide the plants with important nitrogen compounds that they need for healthy growth.

A slide of these bacteria can be made in this way. Select a small nodule about the size of a pin-head. Crush it between two clean slides that are moved against each other so that the nodule material is smeared over a large part of each slide. Try to spread out the material as much as you can. Then, fix one of the slides in a flame, in the usual way, and stain with methylene blue. When you examine the bacteria under the high power, you will notice their somewhat unusual shape. Most of them will appear rod-shaped. Some, however, seem to have a little bump or projection; others may appear Y-shaped.

Fig. 41. Bacteria clinging to the roots of a peanut plant.

SAUERKRAUT BACTERIA

Do you like sauerkraut? It is made by the action of another type of useful bacteria on cabbage. You can see living bacteria by looking at a drop of sauerkraut juice.

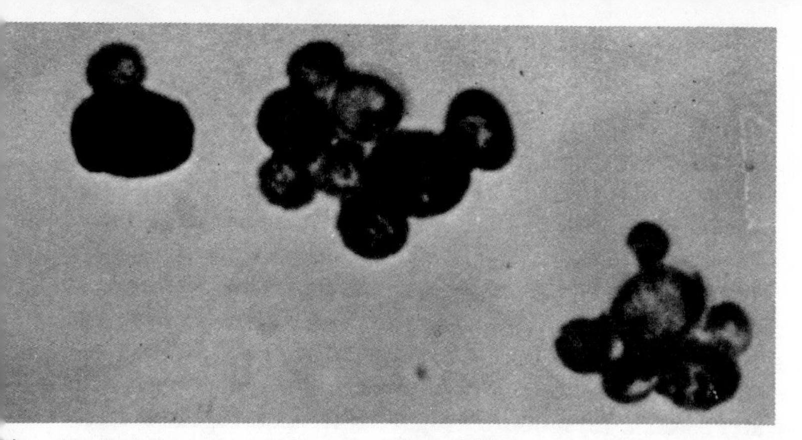

Fig. 42. Budding yeast cells (magnified 1000x).

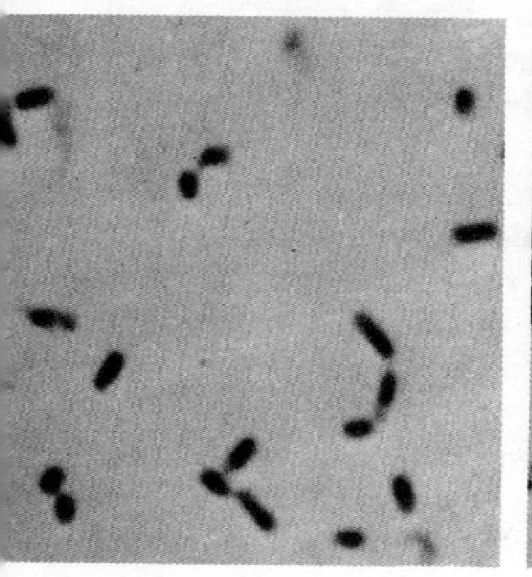

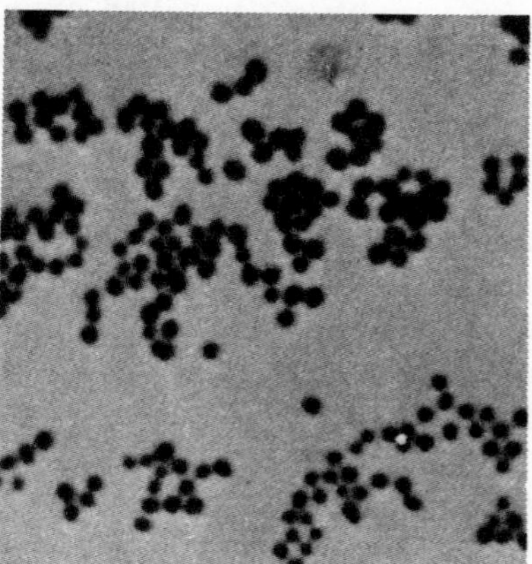

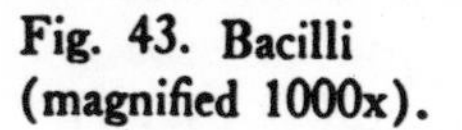

Fig. 43. Bacilli (magnified 1000x).

Fig. 44. Staphylococci (magnified 1000x).

Courtesy of Herbert A. Fischler

Place a drop on a clean slide, and cover with a cover slip. Reduce the amount of light somewhat, so that you can see the bacteria which will be colorless. You will see them twisting and turning about. Some move in a straight line for a short distance and then seem to disappear as they go down a little deeper in the drop just beyond view. To follow them, turn the fine adjustment of the microscope downward.

XI

YEAST AND MOLDS

BAKING YEAST

The yeast cake that your mother uses in baking contains thousands of tiny plants, each so small that you would need a microscope to see it. To study some yeast cells, crumble a small piece of a yeast cake into a glass of water; add a teaspoon of sugar to it. The sugar is used as food by the yeast plants. As they use up the sugar, they give off a gas called carbon dioxide which you can see bubbling upward in the solution, after a few hours. The yeast plants grow especially rapidly if you put the jar in a warm place.

The following day, put a drop of the solution on a slide. Add a drop of water to this liquid, and put a cover slip over it. There are so many yeast plants on the slide, that unless you dilute them with this drop of water, they will be too close together for you to be able to make out their structure.

Under the low power, all you can see will be tiny cells, so small that they appear to be mere dots. Each of these is a yeast plant or cell. When you turn to the high power, you can see a little more detail about the structure (see *Figure 42*). If you look carefully, you can see a clear area in each cell. This is a vacuole, and is usually filled with food material that is stored by the cell. Attached to many of the yeast cells, you will see tiny projections or buds. As a yeast cell grows, it begins to divide, and pinch off a little part of itself to form a new cell. This method of reproduction is called budding. Sometimes, there may be many buds attached to a larger mother cell.

Yeast is useful in the baking industry because it gives off carbon dioxide, and makes dough rise. Without this action, the bread we eat would be hard-packed and too solid. It would lack the fluffiness caused by the presence of many air spaces. Yeast is also used in the brewing industry because of the action of yeast on sugar to produce alcohol. These two products, carbon dioxide and alcohol are formed by yeast during the fermentation of sugar.

BREAD MOLD

Another interesting small plant is the mold that grows on bread or other food. Most people do not suspect that this mold is a plant that has an interesting history of development. You can study this in the following way: Put a piece of moist blotter in the bottom of a jar. Add a small piece of bread. Now sprinkle some ordinary household dust onto the bread. Seal the jar tightly so that none of the moisture can evaporate. Observe the jar every day for a period of a week and a half.

At first, there seems to be nothing happening. Then, on the second or third day, you will suddenly see some cottony material on the bread. The next day, there will be more of it. This fuzzy, white material will seem to be spreading. A few days later, little black dots will be visible, scattered throughout the fuzz. You will now be able to recognize the mold that has developed on the bread.

To see what this mold looks like under the microscope, prepare a slide by taking a small amount of the mold off the bread or the side of the jar with a pair of forceps. Do not take too much of this material; the slide would become too crowded to reveal anything. Add a drop of water, and cover with a cover slip.

Now the plant can be seen to possess a large ball-like structure at one end. It contains many tiny little cells called spores. In making the slide, you may have broken one of these spore cases, and the spores may be all over the slide. These spores are so small that they cannot be seen without the aid of a microscope. Move the slide and trace the long stem-like structure to which the spore case is attached, until you come to the bottom. Here, you can see the root-like structure which anchors the mold to the bread. From these roots, the food is absorbed into the mold, enabling it to grow (see *Figure 45*).

You may wonder how the mold appeared on the bread in the first place. The dust that you sprinkled on the bread undoubtedly contained many spores. These spores are present everywhere, in dust, in the air, and in the soil. When they have the right conditions of moisture and food, they will germinate and form the mold plant.

THE PENICILLIN MOLD

The ordinary bread mold that we have been discussing is black. Sometimes, a blue-green mold appears on bread, or fruit that has been left in a moist place. This blue-green mold has become quite famous in recent years, because it gives off the substance known as penicillin. The mold itself is called *Penicillium notatum*. It is very common, and was used commercially for many years in making the so-called blue-green cheese, or Rocquefort cheese, before it became famous in medicine. This mold gives the cheese its particular flavor and color.

Under the microscope, *Penicillium* looks a little different from bread mold. Instead of the spores being formed in a round spore case, they appear at the ends of branches, like grapes in a row. These spores, too, are present practically everywhere. When the record stratosphere flight was made in a balloon a number of years ago, it was found that mold spores were present in the atmosphere twelve miles up. They were unaffected by the intense cold because of their heavy protective wall. When these spores were brought down and placed in an incubator, they germinated into mold plants (see *Figure 46*).

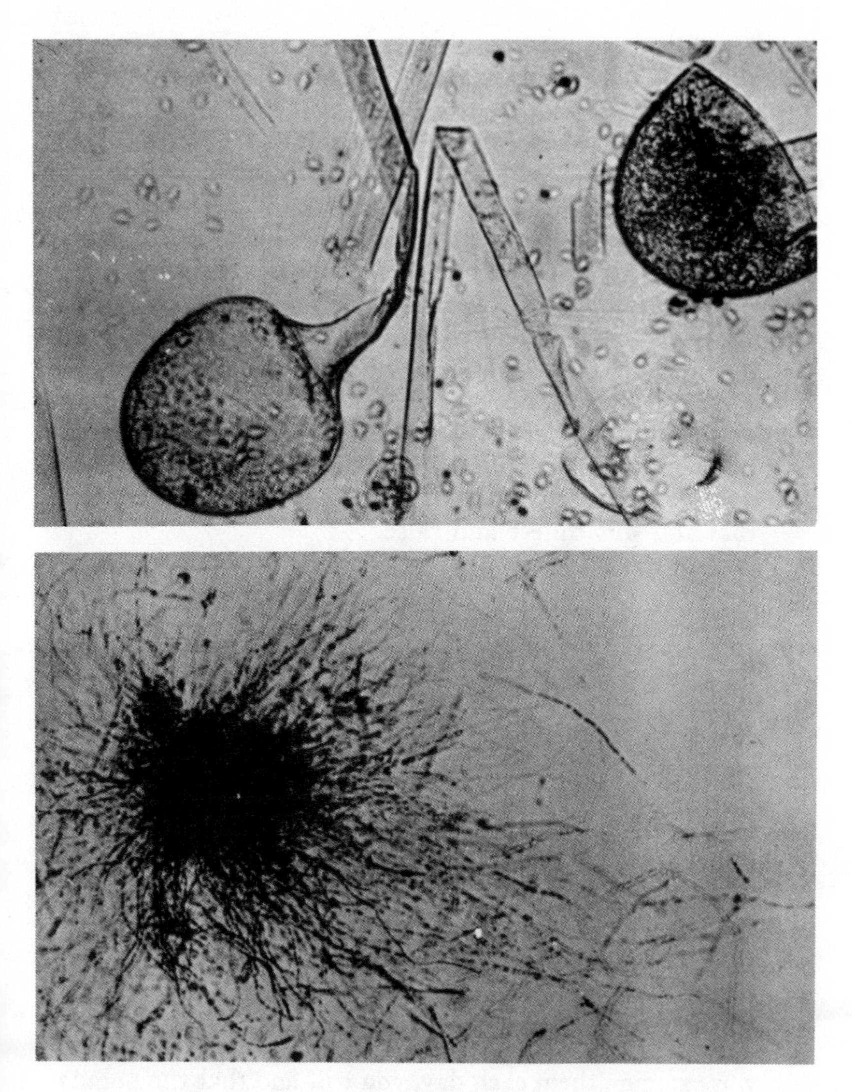

Fig. 45. *Upper photo:* Bread Mold (magnified 100x).
Fig. 46. *Lower photo:* Penicillium Mold (magnified 87x).
Courtesy of Herbert A. Fischler

XII

YOUR MICRO-GARDEN AND ZOO (PREPARING CULTURES)

As you become better acquainted with the strange world revealed by your microscope, you will want to keep a collection of the microscopic animals and plants for future study. The continuous changes in the lives of the captives in your zoo, their rapid multiplication, their struggles for existence, and their surprising activities will furnish many absorbing hours of instruction and entertainment for you and your friends. To establish a zoo, all you need will be a few simple jars and materials for handling the animals that you will collect and raise.

You have already learned how to collect microscopic big game from the ponds and streams (see pages 48-74). When you return home, remove the lids from your collecting jars (see Fig. 47). Place the jars on a window sill, but protect them from direct sunlight. Some animals can be found in the jars almost immediately. Others will make their appearance in 24 to 48 hours. Most of them will gather at the top of each jar, where they can be collected easily with a medicine dropper. Different kinds of microscopic animals will be found an inch or two beneath the surface, and still others, such as Amoeba, will cling to the bottom of the jar. Explore all these areas with your microscope to find inhabitants for your zoo. Take samplings from different areas, put them on separate well-slides, and try to identify them under your microscope.

You should keep your jars for a number of weeks. As you examine them each day, you will find that the population will change. Some types of animals will die out. Others will appear and multiply. In this way, you will have a steady supply of new animals for your microscopic zoo.

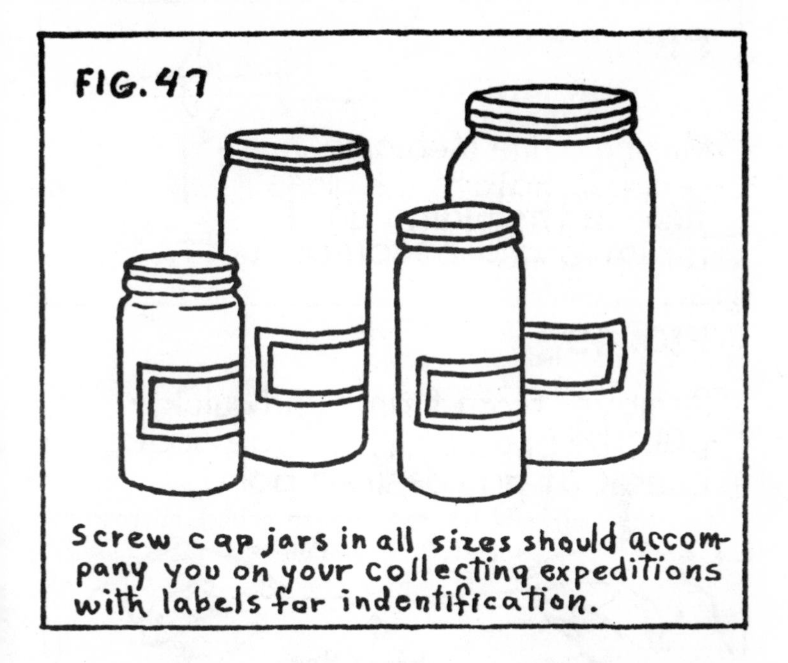

FIG. 47

Screw cap jars in all sizes should accompany you on your collecting expeditions with labels for indentification.

HOW TO TRANSFER ANIMALS TO NEW HOMES

When a particular type of animal appears to be at the height of its numbers in a jar, it becomes necessary to transfer it to a new container. This is usually done in such a way, that only that particular type of animal is to be present in the new jar. This is easier if you have medicine droppers with fine-pointed tips. The soft glass of a medicine dropper can be melted quite easily over a gas flame. Heat the middle of the dropper until it is soft (see Fig. 48). Then remove it from the flame. Holding each end in the tips of your fingers, quickly pull in opposite directions until the glass is drawn out to a fine tube (See Fig. 49). Now simply break it at any desired point and you have a fine collecting tube. This can easily pick up a single animal as you watch it under the microscope. If that one

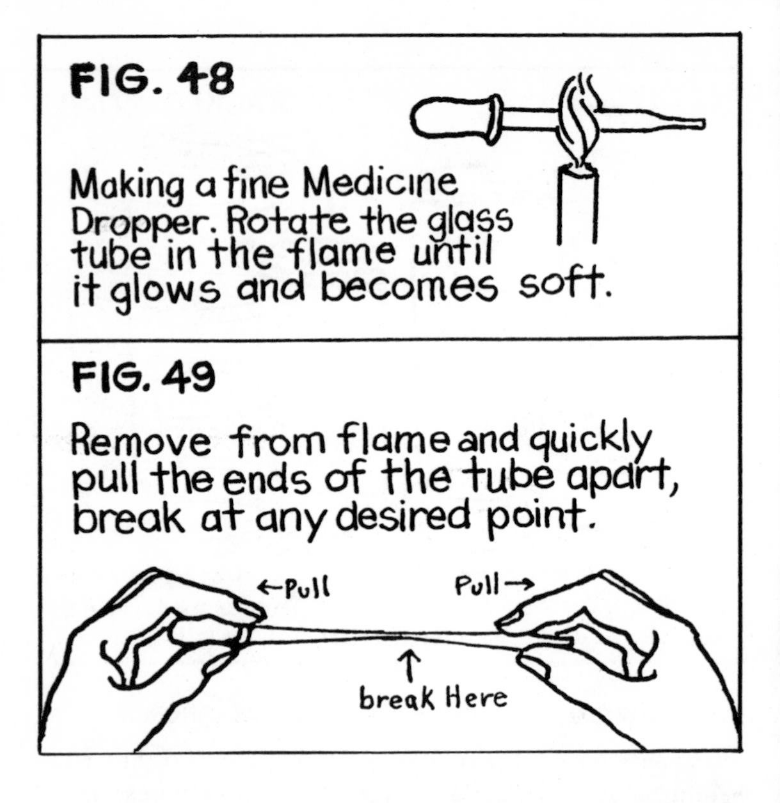

animal is now placed in a new jar containing the proper food material, it will quickly multiply and soon you will have many thousands, all of the same kind. Instead of using jars, you may wish to purchase special culture dishes from your biological supply store. There are two kinds of dishes. The *finger bowl* (see Fig. 50) is a large container which holds a full cup (8 ounces) of liquid. The *Syracuse dish* (see Fig. 51) is smaller. It holds only a teaspoonful or two, but it can be placed directly on your microscope stage for direct examination (see Fig. 53). Both types can be stacked one on the other for convenient storage (see Fig. 52).

FIG. 50
STACKED BOWLS
FINGER BOWL
FIG. 51
SYRACUSE DISH
FIG. 52 STACKED DISHES
FIG. 53
Place the material to be examined in a shallow dish under the microscope. When you see an animal in which you are interested, Fish for it with your fine medicine dropper.

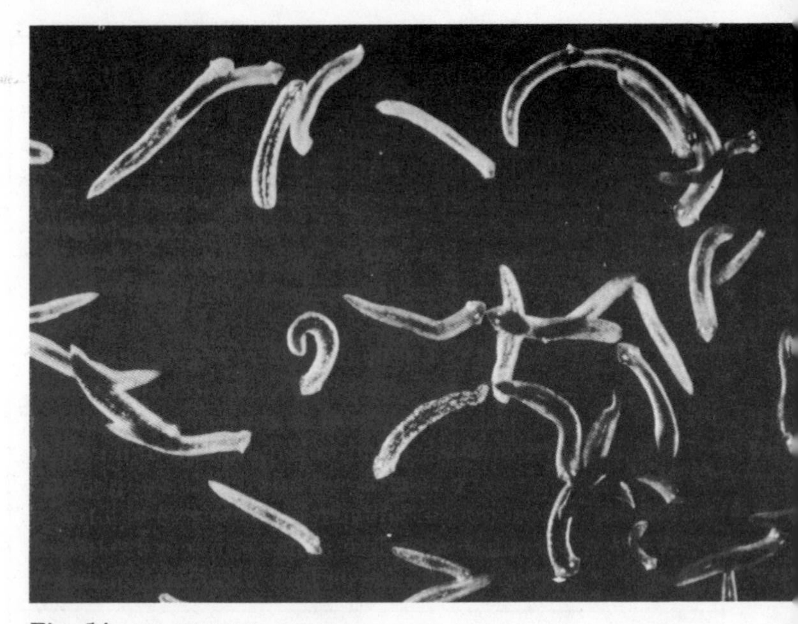

Fig. 54. PLANARIA WORMS IN THE ZOO
Courtesy of Carolina Biological Supply Co., Burlington N.C.

The Planaria (see Fig. 54) is a little flat brown worm, less than half an inch long. It may be found under stones in ponds, or on the bottoms of water lily pads, or leaves of other water plants. It may also be collected by tying pieces of raw meat to strings and letting them lie in the water. Place the worms in a white dish in about an inch of water. Every week, feed them with a very small piece of fresh liver. The worms will attach themselves to the meat and should be removed after an hour. Remove the meat after feeding. Change the water each day, adding fresh pond water.

There are several very interesting and instructive experiments that anyone can perform successfully with Planaria worms. Can you get worms with two heads or two tails? Try the following experiments by making different types of cuts (see Fig. 55) and see what happens:

Experiment 1. To grow a worm with two tails, simply make a cut lengthwise with a sharp razor blade as shown by dotted line in Diagram 1.

Experiment 2. If you want a worm with two heads, first cut off the worm's head as shown in Diagram 2; then, make a short lengthwise cut as shown in the same diagram.

Experiment 3. Cut a Planaria worm into 8 pieces, as shown in Diagram 3. Place each piece in a separate Syracuse dish of water and label the dish so that you can tell which section of the body each piece came from. It is not always possible to predict the results of this experiment, but it will produce some strange and interesting creatures.

Experiment 4. Make two diagonal cuts as shown in Diagram 4. The center section will grow a head that will come out at an angle, and a tail that will also grow out at an angle.

Experiment 5. Remove the head at cut 1, and then cut out a triangular piece as shown in cut 2. A normal head will develop at cut 1, and a smaller head at cut 2.

In all cases, after you have made your cuts, place the worms in a dish of clean water. Sometimes the edges of the cuts may start to grow together again. If they do, simply repeat the cuts you made the first time. The process of regrowth may be slow, but be patient. Do not make the mistake of thinking the worms are dead if they do not move after their operation. Continue taking care of them until you have your unusual new specimens. Undoubtedly, you will want to keep a record of these experiments, and you might make sketches of the results.

Use the lowest power on your microscope or a pocket lens when you perform these experiments, and when you view the Planaria in the process of regrowth.

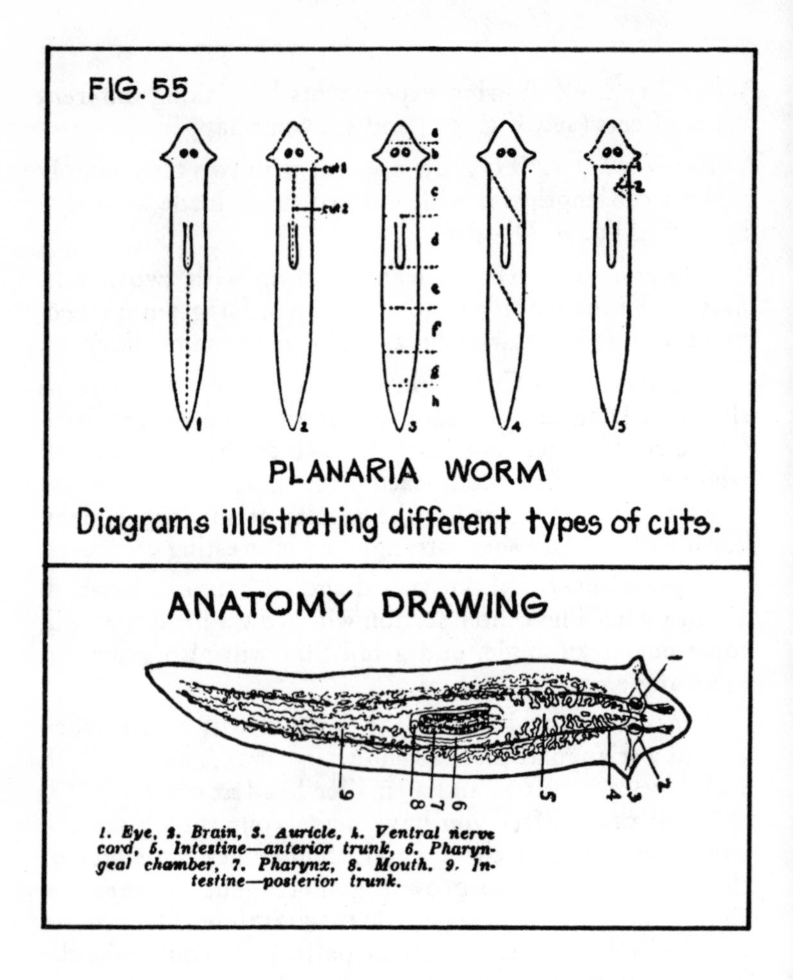

THE FAMOUS FRUIT FLY

The little fruit fly (see Fig. 56) has become a well-known character because it has been used to study the laws of heredity. You will find it a fine addition to your zoo because you can use it to study such insect parts as the wings, the compound eyes, and the legs. The flies are easily captured by placing very ripe pieces of banana in

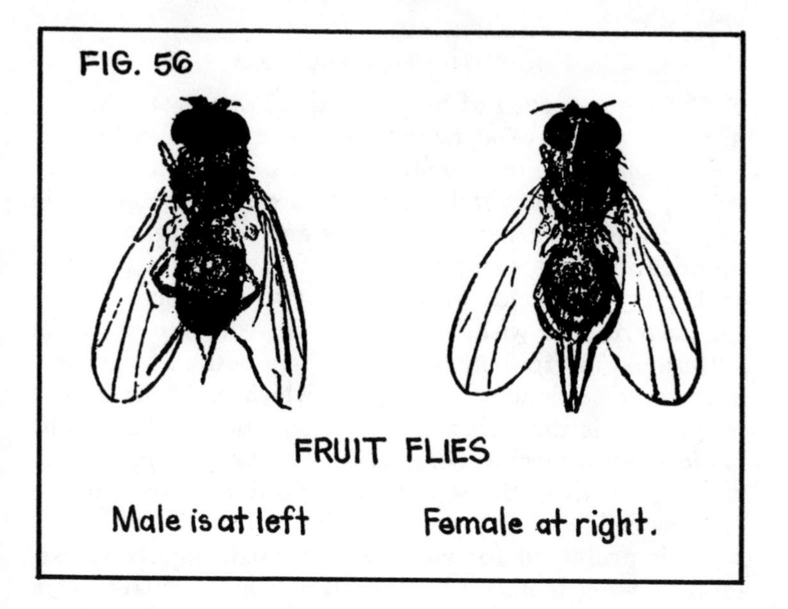

a wide-mouthed bottle and leaving the bottle in a fruit store for an hour or two. After you have obtained your flies, stopper the bottle with cotton. Transfer them to new bottles containing banana from time to time. To make slides of a fly's wing or leg, see page 46.

A GARDEN OF ALGAE

Algae (see Figs. 16, 18 and pages 57, 58) can be grown in the same way as amoeba and its relatives. However, they are very sensitive to poisons and cannot be grown in metal containers. Try making a food supply by boiling a teaspoonful of soil in a quart of pond water or aquarium water. Such algae as desmids and diatoms (see pages 58-60) will grow in this liquid. Some cultures of algae grow slowly and should be kept sealed. Since they are green plants, they need a good supply of light.

HOW TO GROW BACTERIA

Making a garden of bacteria can be done with the few materials you have at home. The basic food is a kind of meat soup. Take one bouillon cube (available at all food stores) and dissolve it in a pint of water. This soup should be placed in small sterilized bottles and sealed with cotton. Sterilization is done by heating the bottles in a pressure cooker at 15 pounds pressure for twenty minutes. Place the bacteria you wish to grow (from your mouth, from buttermilk, or from other sources) in a bottle of the soup. This must be done with a needle which has been heated by passing it through a flame. A suitable needle can be made from nichrome wire, which you can get in a hardware store. Keep the soup in a warm dark place and the bacteria will multiply rapidly. Although a 1000x microscope is preferred for viewing such small objects as bacteria, a 500x is also adequate. If the bacteria are large enough, there's a possibility of seeing them through a 300x microscope.

XIII

DETECTING POLLUTION WITH YOUR MICROSCOPE

Nowadays we are all aware of our environment and the harmful substances that have been poured into the soil, air, and water. But being aware of pollution is not enough; we must also be on the alert for the spread of pollution because of the many ways it can harm us. You and your microscope can be very useful in detecting this menace. You might, for example, be able to prevent a healthy fresh-water pond or lake, with plenty of good fishing, from becoming a lifeless body of water where no fish can survive.

One type of water pollution is caused by nitrates seeping into the water from fertilizers and phosphates present in household detergents. These harmful chemicals overfertilize a pond or lake. Overfertilization can destroy pond life as follows: five hundred forty grams of phosphates can grow 318,000 (318 kg.) of algae. This can be a source of water pollution, since when the algae die, they sink to the bottom and decay. During the process of decay, oxygen is used up until there is no oxygen available for the other forms of life in the water. By sampling the various kinds and numbers of tiny creatures in the mud at the bottom of the lake or pond, you can get a good idea of the degree of pollution there. If you were to compare your findings with surveys of the same body of water made over a period of time even as long as several years, you can tell how well or poorly the body of water is doing, or if the pollution is increasing or decreasing.

If the pond is doing well, there will be few sludge worms present in the mud, and many insect larva such as May flies seen on the surface of the water. May flies lay their eggs in water and their larvae spend two or three years under the sediment of ponds (see *Figure 57*). However, if the oxygen content of the water is reduced, sludge worms (*Tubificids*)

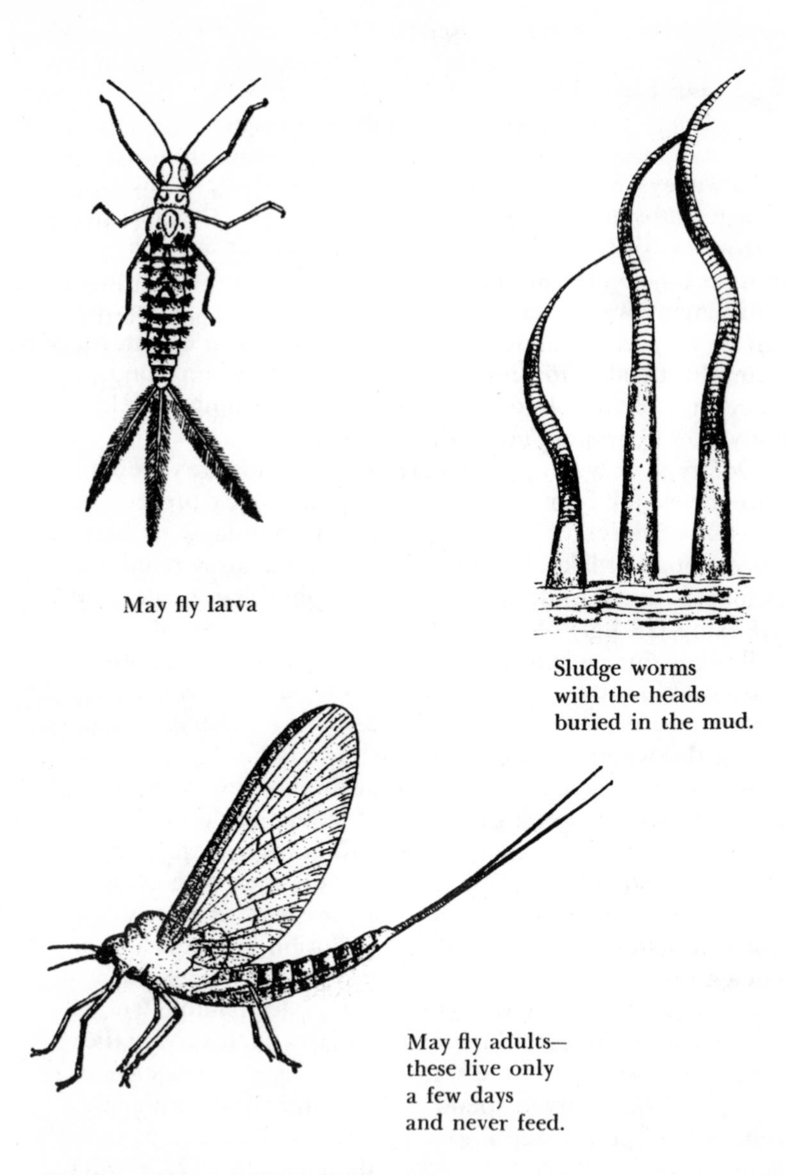

Fig. 57. Living indicators of pollution in ponds.

will be found in great numbers. Their heads will be found buried in the mud with their tails sticking out waving in the current (*Fig. 57*).

Sewage also lowers the available oxygen in a lake or stream because the bacteria that break down the wastes in the sewer use up the oxygen. Sewage bacteria in our drinking water can cause several serious diseases such as typhoid fever or dysentery. Constant checks are made of our drinking water for the presence of the coliform bacteria, normally found in the intestines of humans and animals. If these bacteria are present, it may mean that raw sewage has found its way into the water supply and the more serious typhoid or dysentery bacteria may also be present. Sewage seeping into a lake or stream can be harmful to anyone swimming there; also the coliform bacteria will use up the oxygen supply, thus killing off other microscopic creatures.

Since the sewage bacteria grow on practically any food source, you can grow them at home if you follow the directions on page 126. At this point, it must be emphasized that this type of pollution investigation must be carried on only under the supervision of an adult who is knowledgeable in bacteriological techniques (your biology teacher for example). Typhoid and dysentery bacteria are serious threats to your health and precautions must be taken to prevent transferring the bacteria you are growing from the cultures to your hands or mouth.

The important thing is not that coliform bacteria are found in a water sample, because animal wastes as well as sewage are sources of these bacteria. What is really important is the number of these bacteria in a water sample taken from a lake, pond, or stream. Health departments have standards, and if the number of bacteria per 10 ml. of water is above that number, the body of water is considered polluted.

This is how the water can be tested for bacteria count: the 10 ml. of water from the aquatic environment is poured into a dish containing food for the bacteria and mixed in a clear jelly called *Agar.* The water sample is spread about the surface of the agar and then the dish is kept in a warm, dark place for a day. The dish is then examined and the number of visible *Colonies* of bacteria are counted. Each colony represents a single bacterium. In a warm, dark place and supplied with food and moisture, a single bacterium will reproduce itself many times in a single day, thus forming a colony of bacteria that can be seen without a microscope. If the colonies are small, flat, and separate from each other, they may be *Escherichia coli,* the most common bacteria living in the intestines of warm-blooded animals including humans. If you attempt to do this at home, be certain that you disinfect your equipment by soaking it in a Lysol of CN solution of the proper strength (read the label for directions) when you have finished. Then wash the dishes, etc, with soap and water.

EXAMINING THE AIR WE BREATHE

Pure air is impossible to find outside of certain carefully filtered laboratories because we are using our air to get rid of some of our wastes. There are two kinds of pollutants in the air: gases and particles. While the microscope cannot detect gases, it can detect solid particles. We can easily trap, identify, and count different kinds of pollutants in the air. Each year about 4,000 grams or more of solid particles fall on each square meter of a city. The technique for trapping particles is very simple. Place a slide coated with a thin layer of oil or petroleum jelly in the open air for a few hours. The technique is described on page 83 and is useful for trapping pollutants as well as pollen grains.

The largest solid particle you can find is *dust*; there will be more dust particles in the air than anything else. If you live in a city, the solid pollutant that ranks second to dust is *soot.* Soot is really very finely divided particles of black carbon and is usually seen clumped into long chains (see *Figure 58*).

Fig. 58. The large particle at the bottom is dust. Long chains of soot are also seen.

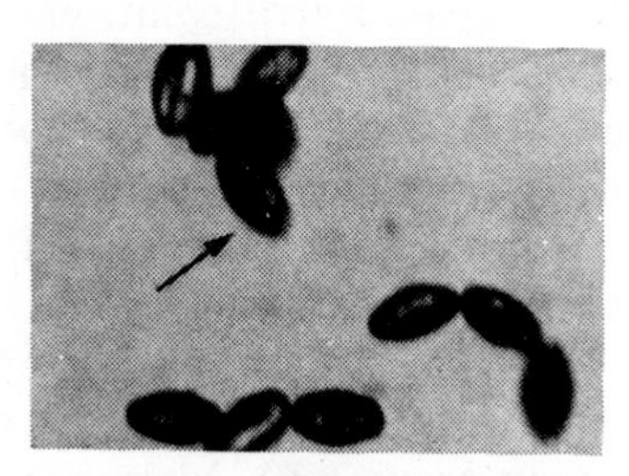

A. Suspected pollen grain shown by arrow.

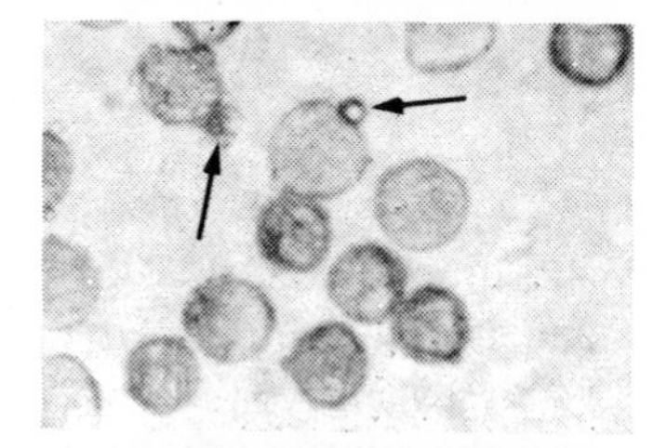

B. Suspected pollen grain after 20 minutes in 10% sugar solution. Note how pollen tubes begin to grow.

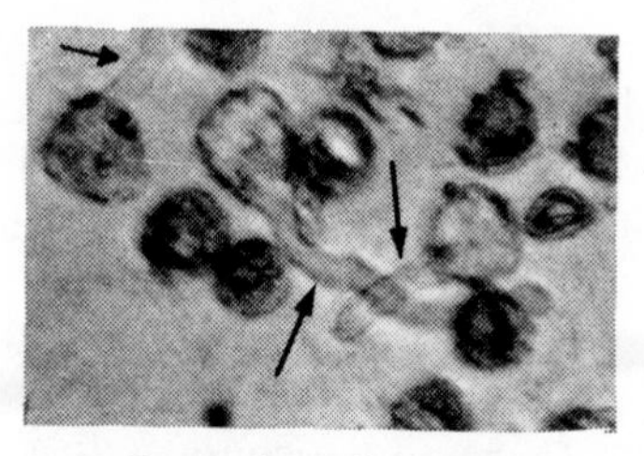

C. Pollen tubes after one hour in sugar solution.

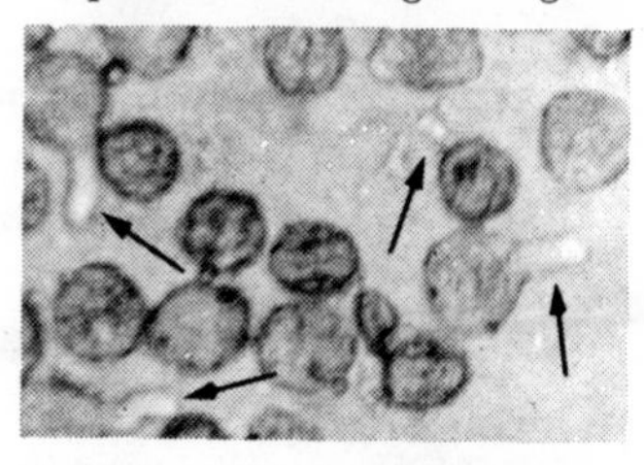

D. Pollen grains after two hours in sugar solution.

Fig. 59. Growing pollen tubes.

In addition to dust and soot, there are many other kinds of solid pollutants in the air, depending upon where you live. You may find lead salts from gasoline or ashes from coal, paper, or wood. Rubber from automobile tires and parts of dead plants may also be blowing around in the air, particularly in the city. Solid pollutants often found in the country include bits of fertilizer, grains, and flour. More pollen will be found in neighborhoods that have fields than in neighborhoods with few or no fields. However, pollen can be carried by the wind for long distances and is a common air pollutant in all kinds of neighborhoods.

If you are not sure whether pollen grains are trapped on your slide, they can be identified as pollen if they form *pollen tubes*. Transfer the suspected pollen grains to a depression slide with a fine needle. Prepare a 10% solution of ordinary table sugar. To do this, dissolve 1 gram of sugar in 10 ml. of water. Mix the solution well before placing a drop of the solution in the depression containing the suspected pollen grains. Cover with a clean cover glass. Examine with the high power of your microscope at 20 minute intervals. Most pollen grains will start to form pollen tubes before 20 minutes have passed, and the tubes will continue to lengthen for two hours or more (see *Figure 59*). Make sure that you add more sugar solution, as the original drop will soon evaporate. A good way to do this is to use a wick technique shown in *Figure 14* on page 43.

The particles in the air of your neighborhood will vary in type and in the amount from day to day and from season to season. Try to compare your daily findings to the local air quality report that is usually included as part of your local weather report.

XIV
ROCKS, MINERALS AND MICROSCOPES

If anyone told you to look at a piece of rock under the high power of a microscope you would probably laugh at the idea. After all, everyone that has ever used a microscope knows that only thin, transparent objects can be seen with the compound microscope. Yet, rocks are examined microscopically every day by geologists because they are looking for valuable ores, such as uranium or gold. In his investigation, the geologist works with a small piece of rock that has been made thin enough to be transparent. Making a rock transparent, however, is a long and painstaking process. First, the geologist uses a special saw blade coated with industrial diamonds to cut a thin chip from the rock. The chip is usually about 2 cm. square and 6 mm. thick. Since you probably don't own a geologist's saw, look for a sample of rock that is close to these measurements. Be sure that the thickness of the rock chip is uniform. One edge should not be thicker than the other.

You can make the surface smooth by grinding and polishing the chip in a thick mixture of fine carborundum powder and water on a glass plate. The chip is rotated in this mixture until the surface is smooth. This takes a long time, possibly days. The chip is than cemented on a glass slide, using Canada Balsam (see page 46). Before cementing, the balsam should be cooked for approximately two minutes at low temperature. When cooled, the drop of balsam should be tough and solid. If you overcook the balsam, it will be brittle and will usually turn brown after cooking. Be sure to center the rock chip upon the slide containing the warm liquid balsam.

After the chip is cemented to the slide, it must be ground down to 0.03 mm. This is the most difficult part because the chip must be ground down evenly, using a carborundum and water mixture on a thick glass plate, as before.

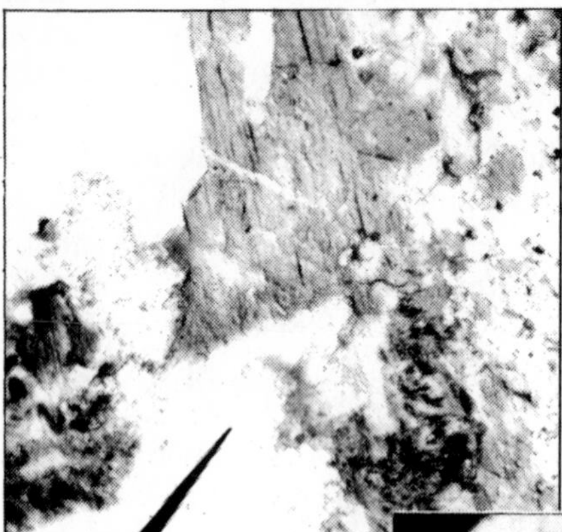

Fig. 60A. A specimen of basalt at 400X. The pointer indicates the specimen's major constituent.

Fig. 60B. A diabase specimen at 400X. The pointer indicates a feldspar concentration. The dark area at the upper right is pyroxine.

Check your progress for transparency every so often with your microscope. When the section is thin enough to be transparent, wash it to get rid of the remaining carborundum. After the section has dried, add more liquid Canada Balsam and a thin cover slip to make it permanent. You now have a microscopically thin section of rock (see *Figure 60*). Using this procedure, scientists have discovered microscopic algae fossils embedded in some of the oldest rock yet discovered.

A word of caution—making rock slides takes lots of time and effort even when professional equipment is available.

Fig. 61A. Salt crystals at 400X.

Fig. 61B. A single sugar crystal at 400X.

COMMON CRYSTALS

It is much easier to prepare chemical crystals than a rock chip for the microscope. The best way to do this is to place a drop or two of a chemical solution on a clean slide and allow the solution to evaporate by applying gentle heat. Sugar, salt, alum, cream of tartar, etc., are a few of the many solutions that will provide excellent crystals for microscopic examination. Crystals can be viewed either dry or mounted in Canada Balsam under a cover glass (see *Figure 61*).

USING POLARIZED LIGHT FOR MICROSCOPIC EXAMINATION

Normal waves of light vibrate in all directions along their path. Imagine a beam of light as a piece of rope tied at one end, with the other end being rapidly shaken up, down, and sideways. A *polarizer* stops the vibrations in all but one direction (see *Figure 62*). This is how polarizing sunglasses reduce glare when the sun's rays pass through the glasses into your eyes. You can use the lenses from polarizing sunglasses for our next experiment or you can buy sheets of polarizing material from a scientific supply house. You will need two polarizers and your microscope. Place one polarizer between the light source and the stage of your microscope (*Figure 63*). The second polarizer should be located between your eye and the eyepiece. To see how

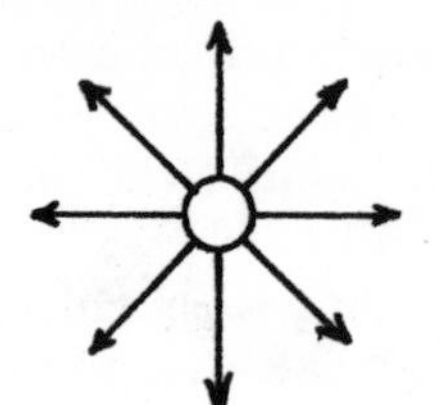

Fig. 62A. Head-on view of vibrations of non-polarized light beam.

Fig. 62B. Head-on view of vibrations of polarized light beam.

Fig. 63A. Benzoic acid crystals (400X), as seen with normal light.

Fig. 63B. Benzoic acid crystals (400X), viewed under polarized light. Unfortunately, the brilliant colors that this causes cannot be seen here.

the polarizers affect the appearance of light, look through the eyepiece at the empty stage and slowly turn the second polarizer (at the eyepiece) while keeping the first polarizer still. Notice what happens to the glaring white light coming up from the light source.

Here is another interesting experiment with polarized light. You will need some clear plastic like that used for packaging small items such as ball-point pens. First twist the plastic until creases appear. Now mount it on the stage of the microscope and get a crease in focus using non-polarized light. Place the two polarized sheets in place on the microscope as you did before. Slowly rotate the eyepiece polarizer and look for color changes in the crease.

Some chemicals and minerals show unusual and fascinating color effects under polarized light. Mica, a fairly common transparent mineral, is one example. Another is the organic compound hippuric acid. Benzoic acid crystals are shown under normal and polarized light in *Figure 63*.

Examine salt, sugar, and even some of the microorganisms in your collection with the polarizers and you may see them in a new light that will astonish you!

XV
IS THERE A MICROSCOPE IN YOUR FUTURE?

We have been looking through the microscope at some strange and fascinating things, both living and non-living. We have hunted plants and animals in the micro-jungle, learned a little about forensic detective work and a little about bacteriology, and we have even done a little surgery. In a word, we have taken that first important step on the road of scientific research.

When you have completed your schooling and begin to earn a living, you may find yourself working at a tedious, tiring, and poor-paying job, or you may find yourself doing something you really enjoy doing, and being well-paid for it. The luckiest people are those who work at something they really enjoy. They look forward to going to work every day and they find their careers rewarding and pleasurable.

Stop a moment and ask yourself: Did you enjoy working with the microscope? Are you curious about the many new things you have seen in this strange micro-world, but do not fully understand? Are your curious to learn more about them?

If the answers to these questions are yes, and if you know how to use the microscope, you might be opening the door to many well-paying and respected occupations and professions. They range from A (Anatomist) to Z (Zoologist). Some of these are shown on the Chart in Figure 64, but there are many, many more that revolve around the use of the microscope than are shown here.

Ask a scientist if he or she enjoys the work. You will probably be told that the scientist never grows tired of it. There is always some unsolved problem that excites their curiosity. There are so many great unknowns waiting to be discovered, so many serious problems facing all of mankind (energy, pollution, cancer, genetic engineering, etc.) that there is no end to interesting work for the scientist.

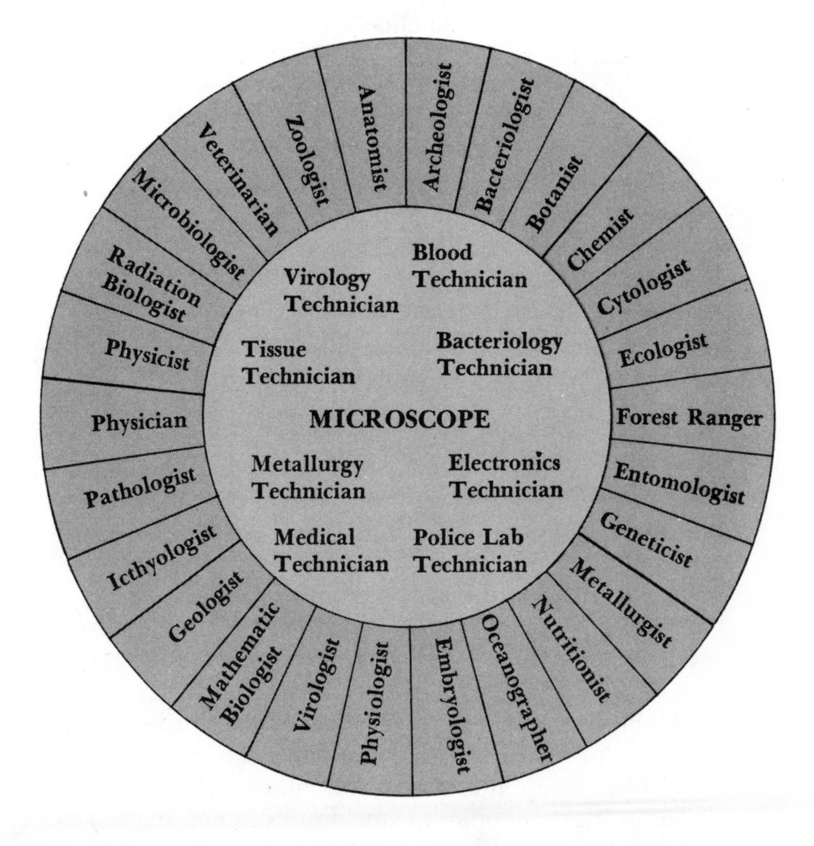

Fig. 64. Possible careers in microscopy. Shaded area represents studies that can generally be completed in a two-year university or community college program.

If you enjoy working with the microscope, now might be the right time to find out if there is a microscope in your future. Some of the world's greatest scientists became interested in science at your age, in just this small way. How do you go about it? When you enter high school, discuss your interest with your science teacher or guidance counselor. They can help you choose the science courses you are best fitted for and those you should take. If there is a microscope club or another kind of science club in the school, join it and take part in the science fairs. There you will meet other students who share the same interests as you. Or you might get in touch with your local science museum. Many of them offer science workshops and clubs for young people. Local colleges sometimes set up special clubs and summer or week-end workshops for interested teen-agers. You will find the college professors ready and quite willing to help young, budding scientists. If you are especially talented you might even earn a scholarship for college.

As you work with your microscope, and as your interest in science begins to grow, you will begin to appreciate the need to get a proper education. Take as many science courses as you can. Everything you learn will be useful later, and the variety of courses will help you become aware of the many scientific specialties open to you.

If you do not go on to a four-year college you can become a lab technician by attending a two-year community college. A few of the many careers in lab technology are shown in the inner circle in Figure 64. If you are fortunate enough to go on to a four-year college and graduate school, even more interesting and varied specialties (and better paying opportunities) are open to you. For example, in the field of microbiology alone, one microbiologist might study only human disease-causing organisms. A second microbiologist may work solely in the field of allergies and immune reactions, while a third might work with a veterinarian, researching diseases of domestic animals. Still another might specialize in fungi or viruses or possibly the genes of bacteria. The list of microbiological specialties goes on and on.

As your knowledge increases, you will be able to make up your mind as to which of the sciences you most enjoy and, possibly, which one you will want to make your life's work. Good luck! And welcome to the ranks of the microscope hunters.

DATE DUE

[illegible]